ANIMATED
OBJECT TALKS

ANIMATED OBJECT TALKS

by

Clyde Foushee

BAKER BOOK HOUSE
Grand Rapids, Michigan

To my daughter

JOYCE

This book is lovingly dedicated

CONTENTS

FOREWORD

THE VERY KIND RECEPTION ACCORDED HIS FIRST TWO volumes of object lessons, *Object Lessons for Youth* and *52 Workable Object Lessons*, has led the author to believe that there is a public demand for a third volume.

The place and purpose of the children's object sermons were fully discussed in the Foreword to each of these two volumes. The author would add here that all the object sermons contained in this book have been preached to the young people of his congregation, and their effectiveness, therefore, has had a fairly practical test. The eagerness with which they were heard by young and old alike leads to the hope that they may reach other children as well.

I am especially grateful to Mrs. Julian Craig, who patiently assisted in the preparation of the material for publication, and to the children and young people of the Second Presbyterian Church of Spartanburg, South Carolina, who listened patiently and attentively to these sermons.

CLYDE FOUSHEE

ANIMATED
OBJECT TALKS

1. THE LAW OF THE UPWARD PULL

TEXT: *If I be lifted up I will draw all men unto me.* JOHN 12:32.

OBJECTS: Four apples. Tie a piece of string about three feet long to the stem of each apple and place an apple on each corner of the table.

THE LESSON: Today we shall demonstrate the law of the upward pull by the use of these four apples. (Gather the loose ends of the strings in your hand and raise your hand above the table until the strings become tight, but not tight enough to cause the apples to move.) You can see that the apples are as far apart as they can be and still remain on the table, but as I tighten the strings, the apples will come closer together. (Lift the apples clear of the table, and they will all come together.)

Jesus once said, "If I be lifted up I will draw all men unto me." Just as the law of the upward pull will bring the apples closer together so all men and women are brought closer together in love and service when they lift up Christ.

Many great and powerful forces are at work in the world today. Many of these forces certainly do not have a tendency to lift men up. War is a powerful force which may lift one nation above another in military victory but it has to do so by beating the other nation down. The only powerful constructive force in all the world which will lift a man up is the love of God working in the hearts of men.

This law of the upward pull applies to everything we do in the work of the church. When we lift up the church by practicing the principles of Jesus we are certainly helping to bring the members of the church into a closer relationship with the ideals of Jesus. I once attended a church meeting from which it seemed that the spirit of God was totally absent. Some of the members lost their tempers and said things which should not have been said. Others were eagerly waiting to respond in kind. And then a saintly old white-haired man walked leisurely down to the front of the church and stood directly behind the communion table. Without saying a word, he raised his hands above his head as if he were about to announce to the congregation that it was time for prayer. A sudden silence fell over the whole group. The old man stood there for fully a minute while everybody waited for him to speak. Instead, he did not say a word. After that tense minute he lowered his hands, and walked back to his seat.

Tempers subsided. The tension was eased, and the spirit of harmony returned. The issue was quickly settled to the satisfaction of everybody. When the old man lifted Christ up, he lifted the spirit of the meeting up to a higher Christian level.

It has been said that when a certain Indian tribe decided to go on a fire-water spree the chief would appoint one Indian to stay sober so that the sober Indian could protect the camp from harm. So when all the Indians got drunk they would have the one sober Indian to protect the camp. My, what a parable that is for our day. Every church needs one sober Indian who will lift Christ up when others may become confused and lose their sense of judgment. When Christ is lifted up the entire congregation is brought closer together and closer to the Kingdom of God.

Christ needs to be lifted up in the home. One of the oldest books of the Bible—the Book of Judges—is the story about one family. One, named Manoah, wanted a son. One day a messenger from God came into the home and told Manoah that God was going to give him a son. As soon as Manoah heard the good news he asked the messenger this question: "When your words come true how is the lad to be trained? What is he going to be?" We older folks are asking that question now about you boys and girls. What are you going to be? Some day you boys and girls will give us the answer to that question and I hope that we all may be proud of the answer you give us.

If there is to be any peace or happiness in your home somebody in the home must endeavor to keep Jesus and His principles lifted above the routine events of life. Ordinarily, we expect the parents to set the religious standards in the home and we thank the Lord for the multitude of parents who do just that. But there are many cases in which boys and girls have done much to lift Christ up in the home.

I am thinking now of a home in which the spirit of Jesus did not abide. The father was a drunkard and the mother did not profess the name of Jesus. None of the five children attended church or worshiped God in any way. When Betty, the oldest girl, was fourteen, she spent a week end with a girl friend who invited her to go to church. Betty accepted the invitation. She liked the church atmosphere and enrolled as a regular member of the Sunday school. Soon Betty was taking her little brother and three sisters to Sunday school with her.

Today Betty is the wife of a missionary and is serving the Lord in South America. Her father is an officer in the church, and her mother is teaching in the Sunday school, and her brothers and sisters are attending church regularly. The whole family was brought to Christ and happiness through the prayers and efforts of Betty, who learned to be a follower of Christ, and lifted Him up in the home.

Now, lifting Jesus up is not as complicated as it may seem. When we accept Him as our Saviour we begin to lift Him up just as He begins to lift us up. We are lifting Him up when we pray to Him, sing to Him, give to His cause, live for His principles, and promote the causes of His church.

A few years ago Irving Berlin told of the glory which came to him after he had written the song, "God Bless America." He wrote that song, not to make money for himself, for all of the profits from that song, and it has sold over a million now, go to the Boy Scouts of America. Irving Berlin was not even born in America. He was born in Russia, under a Czar. He came to America in a cattle boat, sold newspapers on the streets of New York, and sang ballads in saloons along the Bowery.

"One night while sitting alone in my room," Berlin said, "I got to thinking of how good the Lord had been to me. Thoughts of gratitude filled my soul. I reached for my pen and wrote 'God Bless America.' The words seemed to come to me without conscious effort. After the song was set to music I knew that it would live in the hearts of men long after my other songs had been forgotten."

The song will live because it came from God—its real author. "If I be lifted up I will draw all men unto me." It is our job to do our best in trying to lift Christ up. After we have done that, then we may leave the results to God.

2. THE IMPATIENT SCOUT

TEXT: *The hand of the diligent shall bear rule: but the slothful shall be under tribute.* PROVERBS 12:24.

OBJECTS: A Toothbrush and a Bible.

THE LESSON: Not long ago a North Carolina Boy Scout was planning to go with his troop on a week's hike and camping trip. Three weeks before time to leave, the scoutmaster gave each of the boys a list of things to take with him in his kit. Among the things were a toothbrush and a Bible.

Soon after the lists were given out, the mother of one of the boys noticed that his toothbrush was missing, and that he had not been taking proper care of his teeth. Somewhat surprised, she asked him where his toothbrush was, and he told her it was safely packed away in his kit, in readiness for the camping trip! The boy was looking forward to it with such anticipation that he had forgotten all about caring for his teeth in the meantime.

When his mother asked about his Bible, he told her eagerly that he had packed that away in the kit too, and would read it after he got to camp.

He is not the only boy to make such a mistake. Sometimes boys who look forward to being doctors or lawyers, ministers, or teachers, business men or airplane pilots when they grow up get so excited about the great things they expect to do that they forget about the months and years they must spend in study and preparation if they are to achieve their ambitions.

They expect just to grow, or drift, into success. But life does not work out that way. The boy who packs his kit and sits down to wait for success is going to be sadly disappointed some day.

Dr. Howard Chidley, who was a noted preacher, once said, "The man who is a successful railroad superintendent today did not pack his kit twenty years ago and wait for a position to open up. He went into the shops and learned all he could about engines.

Then he became an engineer or fireman, then a conductor and so on until he knew the business thoroughly. After those years of hard preparation he became president of the railroad company."

I frequently hear men talking about the good luck that other men seem to have. There is such a thing as luck, boys, but in nine cases out of ten, if you look back of what men call good luck, you will find years of hard work and preparation behind it.

Once there was a king who became worried because so many of his people complained about their bad luck. The king dressed himself like a poor man so that no one would recognize him, and went out to see if he could learn the meaning of the phrase, "bad luck." After he had made his survey and was back in the palace and in his royal robes, he sat alone to think over what he had seen and heard. At last he said to himself, "I believe that bad luck is a phrase used to describe the lazy and indifferent. But I'll test my theory to see if it is correct."

The next morning the king sat beside his window and kept his eye on the road that ran by the palace. The object of his special interest was a large stone lying right in the middle of the road. Soon a farmer came along in an ox cart, but he did not attempt to move the stone. He drove around it, complaining as he went. Then came a soldier, who was happy in the thoughts of the brave deeds he was going to do. He was thinking so much about himself that he did not see the stone until he stumbled over it and fell flat in the dust. He got up, dusted off his uniform, and went on his way, grumbling over the stupid people who had not moved the stone.

So things went on for three weeks, and the stone lay in everybody's way and everybody grumbled because somebody else had not moved it. Then the king sent out a message telling everybody to appear at the palace gates to hear an important proclamation. At the appointed hour the populace gathered in front of the palace.

"My friends," said the king, "that stone you see lying in the middle of the road in everybody's way has been there for months but no one would stoop down to move it. All you did was to grumble about it. I put the stone there myself. Now, see."

The king moved the stone, and the people saw an iron box in the dust where the stone had been. Then the king held up the box and asked a man near by to read the inscription on it. The man read: *This box of gold belongs to him who moves the stone.* And then the king said, "I am convinced that bad luck is just a phrase used to describe those who are too lazy to stoop down and move stones which obstruct their pathway."

These two objects boys and girls—a toothbursh and a Bible—are very important articles, made to be used now. Instead of putting them away for another time, make use of them today—and every day.

3. FINDING YOUR LEVEL IN LIFE

TEXT: *Thou wilt keep him in perfect peace, whose mind is stayed on thee: because he trusteth in thee.* ISAIAH 26:3.

OBJECTS: Two milk bottles half-filled with colored water, and a small rubber tube running from one to the other. Place one end of the tube in a bottle and suck the tube full of water before placing the other end in the second bottle, or the experiment will not work.

THE LESSON: All of you, perhaps, have heard the story of the city woman who on a visit to her country friend was horrified to see a little pig wallowing in a mudhole. She put the pig in the bathtub, gave it a good scrubbing, powdered its nose, sprayed perfume behind its ears, tied a bow of ribbon around its neck, and cautioned it to be a nice, clean little pig. But as soon as she released it the pig went straight back to its mudhole and began to wallow again.

A good juicy mudhole is on the level with a pig's thinking, and, of course, this pig sought its own level. Boys and girls act in the same way, but on different levels. A good boy will find his friends among good boys and girls and a bad boy will go to bad boys for company.

As water seeks its own level, so do human beings. Here we have two milk bottles, each half filled with water, and a rubber tube running from one to the other. Through the tube the water will flow from one bottle to the other in order to find its level. (Place the two bottles together one above the other, watch the water as it runs through the connecting tube until the water level is reached. Show how boys and girls seek their own level.)

"Birds of a feather flock together." That is an old quotation, but it is just as true of human beings as it is of birds. When a new boy moves into a community he will soon seek and find friends among the neighborhood boys who think and act as he thinks and acts. If he is a fine Christian boy who loves truth and honor, he will not be attracted by boys of bad character. Neither will the local juvenile delinquents care very much for his friendship.

I once heard the owner of a chain of hamburger stands say that he could easily determine the character of any one of his hamburger-stand managers by watching the type of people he attracted to his place of business. A vulgar manager would attract vulgar customers. A high-type manager would attract high-type customers. That is true of every walk of life.

Now, the purpose of these stories is to teach you to maintain high standards of conduct. There are three steps by which you can do this.

The first is to accept Jesus as your Saviour. You will

find that as you learn to love Him, you will tend to become like Him, for it seems to be a rule of nature that, consciously or unconsciously, we become more and more like those whom we love. When two old people live together for a long time it is amazing how much alike they become in their thinking and actions. Sometimes a man will wear an old hat—women never do that—until the hat seems to be a part of him.

The second step is to study God's Word. There we learn that those who sin must suffer for it. The record is clear. The best of God's leaders did not escape suffering for their sins. But they constantly tried to do better. One day we see Jacob stealing his brother's birthright, but the next day we see him dreaming of a ladder which reaches all the way to heaven, with angels going up and down it. One time we read of David resorting to all kinds of sinful thinking, and then we read of him sitting heartbroken over the death of his son Absalom. There is Peter denying that he had ever known the Saviour, but afterward he is filled with remorse, and he goes out to proclaim the gospel. As we study the character of the great men and women of the Bible we see that their love for God was always strong enough to help them keep their standards high.

The third step is to form the habit of public worship. The company of other believers strengthens our own faith and helps us to climb the steep ascent to heaven. By taking these three steps, then, our thinking will become more like the thinking of Jesus

Christ, and we will be able to maintain the highest level of conduct.

4. CLOCK-AND-CALENDAR CHRISTIANS

TEXT: *Let every soul be subject unto the higher powers. For there is no power but of God: the powers that be are ordained of God.* ROMANS 13:1.

OBJECTS: An alarm clock and a calendar.

THE LESSON: These two objects—an alarm clock and a calendar—are not very exciting or romantic objects, and yet they are the instruments by which many faithful Christians measure their devotion to God. If the calendar says that it is Sunday, they will look at the clock, and when it is time to start, they will be on their way to church.

They may not always feel like going to church on Sunday morning, but they will go just the same. They never wait for urges or visions or hunches. They realize that the church, which is rightly called the house of God, has to be run by human beings who suffer from all sorts of weaknesses. They do not attend church with the hope or the expectation of being swept off their feet by some irresistible impulse. The calendar says that it is Sunday, and the clock says that it is time to go to church, and they begin to put on their coats.

Clock-and-calendar Christians are the salt of the earth. The calendar says that the Thanksgiving season is approaching, and the clock-and-calendar Christian begins to think of the many things for which he is thankful. His feeling of thanksgiving does not begin and end in pious thoughts and empty words. He begins to think of the things he might do to promote the spirit of Jesus in the church, in the community, or in the world. He may think of the hundreds of orphan boys and girls who are depending upon his church, or denomination for a love which will enable them to enjoy some of the necessities of life. Then instead of thanking God that his own children are not as unfortunate, or as poor as these orphans, he thanks God for an opportunity to contribute to a noble cause.

The weeks pass and his calendar reminds him that the Christmas season is approaching. He may not feel like sharing in all of the joyous festivities about him, but his calendar says that Christmas is just around the corner, so he gets busy and revises his old list of friends to whom he will send Christmas greetings. Then when he thinks of how Jesus was born in a manger, he is reminded of the poor people in his own community, and he resolves to brighten their lives by sending them a Christmas basket.

When his calendar reminds him that the season of Easter is approaching, he begins to think of the crucifixion and the resurrection of Jesus, and again he is inspired to follow some course which will make the living Saviour more real, both to himself and to those with whom he may be associated.

When the calendar says that it is time for a specific gift to foreign missions, he does not wait for some emotional experience to move him. He contributes to foreign missions because he knows the world missions board of his church must have money on which to operate. He believes that the church is the most important institution in the world, and that it is his Christian duty to support its causes.

The clock-and-calendar Christian may not seem as colorful and exciting as those who are moved by their emotions, but they are usually the people that keep the churches going. It never occurs to them to wait until the spirit moves them. If money is needed for any cause, they give to that cause without question. If a service is to be rendered, they accept the challenge and do the best they can.

If the minister's sermon does not always inspire and lift them, they never complain. If the minister does not do all of the things they wish he would do, they pray for him and trust that God will lead him to do what he ought to do. They know that it is impossible for any minister to ring the bell every time he gets up to preach, and they do not expect the impossible. They know that if only they will be patient and be in the pew the next Sunday and every Sunday, that God will bless them and lead them nearer to the kingdom of God.

The "airish saints" may come and go, but the good old clock-and-calendar Christians, like Tennyson's babbling brook, go on forever. They bring hope and joy to the heart of every minister, because he knows that they are the real pillars of the church, on whom he can count when the rains descend and the storms come and the winds blow.

You boys and girls have golden opportunities to become clock-and-calendar Christians. We older people are set in our ways. Years of habit forming have set us in our own opinion so that we do not want to change our way of thinking, or our way of doing things. You boys and girls are young. You can quickly adapt yourself to new situations. Your minds are open to new ideas. Habits of long standing do not have to be broken to establish new ones. You can start out with a clean slate.

Great experiences in life come to those who have formed the habit of regular church attendance. Christians who form the habit of worshiping God by the clock and calendar, will get more out of their religion than those who are moved by inner urges.

Prayer is a form of worship which should be practiced with regularity. There are times when we are just not in the mood for prayer, but if we pray only when we feel like it, the time will come when we will not feel much like praying at all. The same thing is true of worship. "As his custom was, [Jesus] went into the synagogue to worship God." Synagogue worship in His day was a cut and dried affair, and I doubt if He got very much inspiration out of such worship. But He was there in His place just the same. And later when He went out to do His work, He went often to the synagogue and preached to the people there.

Now let's take one last look at these two objects—the clock and a calendar—and see how they may be used with great profit in helping us to form better habits of worship. I have a lot more which I would like to say on the subject, but the clock says that it is time for me to stop and I shall obey its timely warning.

5. DON'T KID YOURSELF*

TEXT: *For if any be a hearer of the word, and not a doer, he is like unto a man beholding his natural face in a glass.* JAMES 1:23.

OBJECTS: A mirror and a Bible.

THE LESSON: On the wall of the palace of Snow White and the Seven Dwarfs hangs a magic mirror. Every day the evil queen peers in the magic mirror. Gazing with pride at her own reflection, she asks:

> "Mirror, mirror on the wall
> Who's the fairest of them all?"

Then the magic mirror replies, "You are the fairest, lady queen."

But as little Snow White grows up, she becomes more and more beautiful, and one day, when she begins to fear that Snow White's beauty may rival her own, the queen goes before the mirror again and asks softly:

> "Mirror, mirror on the wall
> Who's the fairest of them all?"

* Adapted from a sermon called "The Parable of the Mirror," by Dr. Paul Tudor Jones and published in *The Christian Observer.* Used by permission of Dr. Jones and the publishers.

This time the answer comes back:

"You were the fairest long ago;
Snow White's the fairest now, you know."

The queen was furious.

We have here a mirror and a Bible, each of which can do more wonderful things for us than any magic mirror could ever do. If you will look into the mirror it will reveal to you how you appear to your friends. When I look into the mirror I see myself as I seem to you. I know that I am not presenting a very pretty picture to you, but I am honestly doing the very best I can. I find great consolation in a little poem I ran across some years ago which runs something like this:

As for beauty, I am no star.
There are many who are better looking by far.
But as for my face, I don't mind it,
    Because I am behind it.
It is the one in front who gets the jar.

The Apostle James says that our Bible is a spiritual mirror which will show us what sort of person we are and tell us the truth about ourselves. Christian believers are fond of saying that the Bible is the revelation of God, that it draws back the curtain of mystery and reveals to man's understanding the nature of God. That is all very true, but it is equally true that the Bible is also a revealer of the nature of man.

James goes on to say that he who reads the Bible and understands what God wants him to do and then does nothing about it is like a man who sees his own reflection in a mirror and then straightway goes off and forgets what manner of man he is.

I am afraid that too many of us, when we read the Bible or listen to a sermon, are looking for the shortcomings of someone else rather than for our own. Recently a mother was telling me how well she thought one of my sermons had hit a good many of our parishioners, when her six-year-old daughter said, "Oh, mother, he wasn't talking to us at all. He was looking directly at all of the people who were sitting up in the balcony."

God's word is like a mirror because it is God's personal message to us. Dr. John Sutherland Bonnell tells of a young business woman in his church who read her Bible consecutively, beginning each day at the place she had left off the previous day and continuing until she met a verse she felt was God's marching orders for that day. Then she would underline the passage, meditate on it, and apply it to every area of life. Next, she would write the verse down on a slip of paper and take it with her for frequent reference. One drab winter morning this young business woman took a taxi to the office where she worked. After a few blocks, the taxi driver leaned back and remarked to his passenger, "New York is a terrible place to live in. Everybody is at everybody else's throat. People's nerves are on edge. The confusion is terrible. A man is crazy to stay in this city if he has any chance of getting away from it."

The young woman smiled and said, "I don't blame

you for feeling that way. I used to feel exactly that way myself."

"Don't you feel that way now?" asked the driver. Then looking directly at his passenger, he said, "You don't look quite like a person who would have religion. Why don't you feel that way now?"

"I don't know," she said, "whether you would call it religion or not, but I have a peace deep down in me which I used not to have."

"How did you get it?" he asked.

"Every time I read the Bible," she said, "I keep on reading until I come to a verse that I feel is God's marching orders for the day. Usually I write this down on a slip of paper and carry it with me. It keeps me steady, whatever happens. It serves as a staff to lean on."

"Did you get a verse today?" asked the driver.

"Yes, I did," she said, "and I have it here. Now it begins to look as though it was intended for you instead of for me. You have been talking about New York being a place of confusion—well, listen to what this says." Opening her handbag, she took out a slip of paper and read these words: "For God is not the author of confusion but of peace" (I Corinthians 14:23).

"Let me see that thing," said the taxi driver, reaching back. The young woman passed him the piece of paper and the taxi driver read it, and passed it back, without a word of comment. They drove the rest of the journey in silence. As she was leaving the taxi, the young woman paid the driver and handed him a tip. Looking at her with a quiet smile on his face, he said,

"Lady, I couldn't take any tip from you. You have given me something this morning worth more than all the tips I can earn today."

Well, you and I can take a tip from the Apostle James. He is telling us something about the Bible which we ought to know. He is saying that it is like a mirror, in that if we will look in it intently we will see not only God but ourselves as well. He reminds us that this book is God's mirror for our souls. We should look into it regularly and pay attention to what it shows us of ourselves and about ourselves. But more, God shows us that here is the storehouse of spiritual strength from which He will supply our daily needs.

This glass mirror will show you what you look like to others. The Bible mirror will reveal to you something of the nature of God, and it will also tell you the truth about yourself. Look into the Bible and quit kidding yourself.

6. LIPSTICK OR PENICILLIN

TEXT: *If ye keep my commandments, ye shall abide in my love; even as I have kept my Father's commandments, and abide in his love.* JOHN 15:10.

OBJECTS: A tube of lipstick and an empty penicillin container.

THE LESSON: This tube of lipstick suggests to me the following parable, which may bring a modern lesson home to us:

Now it came to pass in those days that a certain woman began to grow frail; her body and nerves were jumpy, and her face pale, and her husband suspected that some deep-seated and dangerous ailment was eating away at her health. Finally, he persuaded her to call a physician.

In due time the doctor arrived, and when he beheld his patient he was aghast, and said, "Lo, thy physical reserves are at a low ebb, thy color is gone from thy cheeks, thy lips are pale, and thy hands are nervous."

And then the doctor gave the sick woman a powder compact and a tube of lipstick and said unto her, "If you will put this rouge on your cheeks and this lipstick on your lips you will look so much better that you will soon forget that you are frail in body and spirit."

The woman took the advice of the doctor, and each day she painted her cheeks and lips, and her ailment grew worse and worse, and, lo, she died. When the man saw that his wife was dead he became embittered, for he felt that the doctor had not done his best. Instead of trying to find the cause of his patient's trouble, the doctor had sought only to improve her appearance.

And the doctor repented and said to himself, "I am an unfaithful physician, for, instead of treating the cause of the disease, I treated the symptoms, and, lo, my patient is dead."

As we look again at these two objects, one a tube of lipstick and the other a bottle of penicillin, we see that each represents a type of religion as well as a school of thought.

A lipstick Christian is one who wants his own religion merely to look good. He talks glibly about winning souls for Jesus Christ, but he seldom wins anybody. He may be the first to make a motion for the group to enter into an evangelistic crusade, but when the time comes to do the work he is apt to find fault with the way the decision card has been printed instead of joining in the campaign. Lipstick Christians are the kind who believe that if they prop up their religion with pious phrases and a lot of words it will look pretty good. Lipstick Christians are always trying to leave a good impression, but their religion is in their vocal cords and not in their blood stream. I once visited a lipstick Christian who was in jail for stealing an automobile. He repeated the Apostles' Creed every day. He could not see that the real significance of the creed should have kept him from stealing the automobile.

The man was confusing a religious form with a Christian experience. We cannot get a real experience of Christ by repeating a creed or by leaving off a set of bad habits. The mere absence of badness does not produce goodness.

This little bottle of penicillin was designed, not to cover up blemishes, but to go to the very seat of an ailment and help nature remove its cause.

The religion of Jesus really heals, in that it goes to the root of the trouble. (Show how Jesus went to the heart of the trouble of Nicodemus, of the rich young ruler, of the woman at the well.)

I hope you boys and girls will let Jesus go to the very heart of your problem. Then you will have a joy that you will want to share with everyone. Jesus will not help you to camouflage your sins, but He will forgive them and will remove the cause.

Look again at these two objects—a tube of lipstick and a bottle of penicillin. One covers up blemishes so that a person may look better than he really is; the other gets at the cause of the blemishes.

Each object is symbolic of a current religion. The lipstick represents the religion of the Pharisees. The penicillin is more like the religion of Jesus, because it seeks, not to conceal the blemishes of sin, but to remove their cause. I hope you boys and girls will choose the way of Jesus.

7. WHEN WE TALK WITH GOD

TEXT: *Ye ask, and receive not, because ye ask amiss, that ye may consume it upon your lusts.* JAMES 4:3.

OBJECT: A disconnected telephone.

THE LESSON: I once heard a minister preach a sermon on the telephone. He picked up the phone, dialed heaven, and had a rather strange conversation with the Lord. He proceeded to tell the Lord who he was and what he wanted the Lord to do about certain conditions down here on earth. Then he hung up the receiver and shouted to the congregation, "Praying to God is just as simple as talking on the telephone."

It was all very impressive, but there seemed to be something lacking in the demonstration. Before the service was over it dawned on me what was wrong with the whole idea. Perhaps I can show you better than I can tell you what was lacking.

I am now going to call the mother of one of you children and tell her a few things that I would like to have her know. (Have a child whose mother is not present give you her mother's telephone number and then pretend to phone the mother.)

"Hello, is this Mrs. Doe? This is——, of the—— Church speaking. I want you to know that we think your daughter Jane is a very fine girl. She is one of our best listeners and we are proud to have her in the Junior Choir. But what I really called you about is this: I would like you to come to church next Sunday and bring me a fried chicken and a chocolate cake and a dozen doughnuts. All your neighbors say that you are the best cook in town, and I have a good appetite and have been yearning to eat some of your cooking."

Now, at least three things are wrong with that telephone call.

1. The telephone was not connected, so Mrs. Doe did not hear one word I said. If I did not know that the telephone was not connected I might believe that

Mrs. Doe would surely come to church next Sunday and bring me what I asked for.

I wonder if some of our praying to God is not like trying to use a telephone which has not been connected. Sin breaks the connection. If there is sin—unrenounced sin—in our hearts we have to get rid of it before we can get in touch with God.

2. The second thing wrong with that telephone call was that my request was selfish. I assumed that I knew exactly what I needed. I did all the talking and did not give the person to whom I was talking an opportunity to express her opinion of my request.

I wonder if we do not often treat God in some such manner. Instead of waiting patiently for God to reveal Himself to us, we just prattle on and tell Him what we think He ought to do for us. "Lord," we say, "I want you to give me [whatever it is]," and then we hang up the receiver without ever waiting to consider whether our wishes are in keeping with God's will.

3. The third mistake was that I tried to shift all the responsibility onto Mrs. Doe while asking her to do something for me. It is much easier to ask someone to give us a fried chicken or a dozen doughnuts than it is to go to work to procure them for ourselves. But no person in his right mind is going to keep on giving us things we ask for without stopping to consider whether we need them. We have no right to call on a friend to do things for us if we are not willing to do the best we can for ourselves.

So when we pray, "Lord, bless our church and fill our empty pews with people and our empty hearts with love," and then do not turn a hand to promote what we are praying for, we are trying to pass the buck to the Lord, while we sit on the sidelines and give Him advice.

It is a mistake to keep on telling the Lord what we want Him to do for us and not wait for Him to tell us what He wants *us* to do. If we insist on reaching God without giving God a chance to reach us we will find ourselves talking into empty space and hearing only the echo of our voice in answer.

8. KEEP YOUR LENSES CLEAN

TEXT: *And the Lord opened the eyes of the young man; and he saw: and, behold, the mountain was full of horses and chariots of fire round about Elisha.* II KINGS 6: 17.

OBJECT: An old pair of eyeglasses the lenses of which have been splotched with white polish.

THE LESSON: The world is divided into two kinds of people—those who wear glasses and those who do not. Those of us who have to wear glasses wish that we did not have to do so, and those who do not have to wear them really do not know how fortunate they are.

Wearing glasses is a constant nuisance, because they are always getting soiled and having to be cleaned. If we neglect them, they will soon become so dirty that we shall not be able to see clearly. The day will look gloomy when actually it is fair. Faces that are clean may look blurred and dirty if we see them through soiled glasses. If we try to read a book, the print looks smeared.

Here we have a pair of glasses which have become slightly soiled. (Put them on and look at the audience through them.) You do not appear as bright and clean through the glasses as you do when I look at you without them. Some of your features are blurred. My vision is not at all clear. Those of us who wear glasses know that we must clean them frequently if we are to see things as they really are. Blue glasses will make everything look blue; red glasses will make everything look red. If my glasses are extremely splotched and dirty, they will make you look splotched and dirty.

Our minds have lenses and they, too, can become cloudy and dirty. It is very easy for them to become smeared with the dust of prejudice, the streaks of envy, or the mud of hate. Then we cannot see people as they really are any more than I can see what you are really like when I look at you through these soiled glasses.

Nothing looks good to us when the lenses of our minds are soiled. We just can't see things as they really are. Pilate let his mind become so beclouded with fear and hate that he turned Jesus over to a mob determined to crucify Him.

But we cannot wash our minds with soap and water. I have seen parents make a child wash out his mouth with soap and water after the child had uttered an ugly word. That might be a fine means of discipline, but washing out one's mouth will never permanently stop the flow of ugly words that are pent up inside.

When our minds become dirty, we cannot see the good and the beautiful as they really are. Even though we may see them, they do not look either good or beautiful.

We cannot wash our minds with soap and water, but there are ways by which the lenses of our minds may be cleaned.

Prayer is one of the most powerful forces in all the world to remove grime and dirt from the lenses of our minds. We cannot pray honestly without beginning with ourselves. We must first ask God to forgive us our sins and shortcomings before we can honestly ask Him to do anything else. I have no right to ask God to do for me what I would like to have *Him* do unless I am willing to do what God wants *me* to do. When the Apostle Paul was converted, he began his ministry by saying, "Lord, what wilt thou have me do?"

After Paul got the lenses of his own mind clean, he saw Christianity in a much different light from that in which he had seen it before.

Also, the study of God's Word will do much to help us clean the lenses of our minds. As we read God's Holy Word we will come upon all kinds of people. Some are good and some are bad. Some are successful and some are failures. We will certainly notice that the great successes of the Bible were men and women who kept the lenses of their minds clean by following God's Holy Word. David said, "The Lord is on my side; I will not fear." Paul said, "He which hath begun a good work in you will perform it until the day of Jesus Christ." James said, "Draw nigh to God, and he will draw nigh to you." The Psalmist said, "Weeping may endure for a night, but joy cometh in the morning." Job said, "Though he slay me, yet will I trust in him."

But listen to what the failures said of themselves. Cain said, "Am I my brother's keeper?" Saul said that people were against him and no one pitied him. Pilate said, "What I have written, I have written." Each one said in action what he had already said in his own soul.

Paul recognized this basic fact when he said, "Whatsoever things are true, whatsoever things are honest, whatsoever things are just, whatsoever things are pure, whatsoever things are lovely, whatsoever things are of good report . . . think on these things."

9. BUTTONS FOR GOODNESS

TEXT: *Render therefore to all their dues: tribute to whom tribute is due; custom to whom custom; fear to whom fear; honour to whom honour.* ROMANS 13:7.

OBJECTS: Several lapel buttons which represent church, Sunday school, or social organizations. Briefly explain the meaning of at least one of them.

THE LESSON: This is an age when many kinds of organizations are giving buttons of merit to their most faithful workers. Such buttons often denote extra loyalty on the part of the wearer. Here we have a button which was recently presented by the president of a large textile plant to an employee who had spent fifty years in the service of the company. The recipient of this button, which is called a badge of honor, was an office secretary who had spent a half century at the same desk. In all of that time she had been away from her desk only four days on account of illness. She certainly deserved a badge of honor.

Recently while attending a church conference, someone suggested that churches might well consider presenting buttons of goodness to the faithful members who had rendered outstanding service to the church. Out of the discussion which followed that proposal, the following objections were offered:

I. CHURCHES HAVE NO WAY OF MEASURING THE GOODNESS WHICH MAY BE IN THE HEART OF A MEMBER

First, there is no such thing as a church apart from the spirit of the members which constitute the church. There may be a church building, but there is nothing sacred about a church building. There is an old church building in Louisville, Kentucky, which for a long time has been used as a house in which whiskey is stored. There are now barrels and barrels of whiskey stored in the same building in which people used to worship God. When the membership of the church moved to a more desirable neighborhood, the old church which was left behind no longer maintained the spirit which made it a church.

When we think of a specific church, we may think of such physical features as the building and furnishings, but we must think of the spirit of the people who support the church. Those who love and support the church are heirs to all sorts of human weaknesses. We are not competent to select the proper persons on whom buttons for goodness might be bestowed.

We have no way of measuring goodness as God must measure it. The only possible way that any of us could measure goodness would be on the basis of the visible evidence at hand. Since we cannot read the human mind or know what goes on in the heart, we cannot measure goodness as God must measure it. A deed which we might believe to be an expression of inward goodness, might, in the sight of God, be wholly mean and selfish. The motive behind the deed is the thing that must determine whether a deed is an expression of good or evil.

We are told that the other disciples agreed with Judas when he found fault with Mary because she broke the alabaster box of ointment at the feet of Jesus. In the estimation of the disciples, her act was extravagant and wasteful, but in the eyes of Jesus it was wise and noble. So because we have no infallible way of knowing what goes on in the human heart, we have no adequate way of measuring goodness by human conduct.

II. THE WRONG PEOPLE WOULD ALMOST SURELY GET THE BUTTONS FOR GOODNESS.

If the church should propose to give buttons for goodness to a number of you boys and girls at the end of the year, some of you might work hard to win such an honor. At the close of the year the judges in charge of selecting the recipients of such an honor would have to base their decisions on your visible conduct during the year. Those of you who had participated in the most programs, and had done the most outstanding deeds, or had been the most popular among the other boys and girls, would most likely win the favor of the judges.

Some few might try harder to impress the judges than to please God. The boys and girls who worked and prayed behind the scenes, but who made little or no impression on the crowd would scarcely be considered at all. In the end the wrong people might receive the buttons for goodness, while the right ones might go unnoticed.

Over the years I have observed that among the old as well as the young, when a person seeks to become an officer in the church or some other position of honor or influence, he seldom makes as faithful a leader as the person who does not seek such honors. When we begin to think in terms of some position of honor, we are apt to forget to think in terms of service.

Such was the case with the disciples when they met with Jesus in the Upper Room. It seems that there was no servant present to dust off the sandals of the guests. None of the disciples cared to assume the position of a servant. Then Jesus took a towel and did the job that the disciples were too proud to do. In so doing He taught them that service and not honor must ever be the central motive of a disciple.

III. GOD'S REWARDS ARE SUFFICIENT.

The honors and rewards which may be bestowed by human hands are temporal and of short duration. They may please and elate for awhile, but they can never bring us the lasting joys of life. But God's rewards are sufficient. Let's look at a few of them.

Peace of mind is a gift of God. When we are at peace with God, we can be at peace with ourselves, our friends, and the world. All of the honor and the medals in the world cannot compensate for the absence of this peace of God.

Self-respect is another great reward of God. It comes as the result of a clear conscience and the assurance that we have honestly tried to live as God would have us live. We cannot respect ourselves if we know that our motives are selfish and impure.

Love is another reward of God. As all of the light in the world comes from the sun, so all the love in the world comes from God. Without love, your home would be a place of misery, or your survival would depend upon your physical strength, and there would be no such thing as love as we know it.

Salvation is the ultimate reward for which we are all

striving, and that too, is the gift of God. So if you boys and girls are fortunate enough to receive buttons of honor for good deeds at home, at school, or at church, receive them with grace and gratitude, but do not expect buttons for the goodness you may do for the Master. Serve God without any thought of rewards, and then the Lord will reward you richly for your service.

10. APPLESAUCE

TEXT: *Let us hold fast the profession of our faith without wavering.* HEBREWS 10:23.

OBJECT: A jar of applesauce.

THE LESSON: If I were to ask any one of you boys or girls what this jar contains you would correctly say, "Applesauce." And I would be pleased with your knowledge. But if one of you were to come up to me at the close of this service and say, "Applesauce!" I might not be so well pleased with your judgment.

Boys and girls often use the term "applesauce" to describe insincere praise, or something which does not make sense or something which is too complicated for them to understand.

Far back in the days of the Old Testament people used slang expressions to describe some of the things which they did not like or did not understand. "Aha" is such a word.

In Ezekiel 25:3-4 we read: "Because thou saidst, Aha, against my sanctuary, when it was profaned; and against the land of Israel, when it was desolate; and against the house of Judah, when it went into captivity; behold, therefore I will deliver thee to the men of the east for a possession, and they shall set their palaces in thee, and make their dwellings in thee: they shall eat thy fruit, and they shall drink thy milk."

In the modern American vocabulary of slang today, what the Ammonites said in the long ago against the land of Israel when it was desolate, against God's sanctuary when it was profaned, was "Applesauce!"

The religion which God offered them did not make sense to the Ammonites because their minds had been dulled by the ravages of sin or because they did not want religion at any price.

Now, much of what we read in the newspapers, hear on the radio, or see in the movies or on our television set is pure "applesauce." It is nonsense at which we may laugh or cry depending on our current mood. We like *Charley McCarthy*, *Howdy Doody*, and many other comical entertainers because they make us laugh, and laughter is a good medicine. They are all right in their place.

But there are at least three subjects to which we must not refer with the term "applesauce."

1. The first is God and His church. Jesus once said to Peter that He would build His church on him and that even the gates of hell could not prevail against it. But Jesus Himself never founded the church as we know it today. He left no book of rules, no articles of

faith, no organization such as we have today, no ordained clergy, and no denominational headquarters. The original Christians consisted of a small group of men and women who suffered and died in the obscure corners of the world. Yet this small group of unlettered men and women established little colonies of Christians which grew and multiplied until the cross on which Jesus died was changed from a symbol of disgrace to the symbol of victory over sin and death.

These early Christians established churches. The churches grew and multiplied. And the church as we know it today is made up of all sorts of people. So long as we recognize God as its head it will never fail.

2. You should never look on worship as "a lot of applesauce." Many boys and girls who attend Sunday school but do not remain for the worship service seldom know the meaning of worship. There are at least two things to observe about worship.

(a) Worship should be regular. We read that it was the custom of Jesus to worship in the synagogue regularly. Mere occasional attendance at church benefits one no more than taking an occasional dose of medicine, when the doctor has prescribed regular doses over a period of time. We all need to worship God regularly.

(b) Worship consists of many elements. There is the element of quietness, the element of music and song, the element of praise, the element of stewardship, and the element of teaching and explaining. The sermon is only a part of the worship. True worship should produce in us a strong desire to seek and to find God's will for us.

3. You should never use an undignified term in speaking of God's Word. There is much in the Bible that you may never understand. But if you will read carefully and prayerfully you will find much of it that you can understand. You will learn that there is a penalty for sin and wrongdoing and that God has provided a Saviour who can save us from this penalty. The Bible is a wonderful book about people who struggled to find God's will for them. It tells of God's patience with, and His love for, mankind.

Finally, from the Bible we get a better idea of what God is really like and of the personality and the teaching of Jesus, whose coming changed the whole world and the course of cilvilization, so that everything is dead from the day He came into the world.

11. THE VALUE OF A THING

TEXT: *How much then is a man of more value than a sheep?* MATTHEW 12:12.

OBJECT: An old, dilapidated Teddy bear.

THE LESSON: "Are you any good, Joyce?" the father teasingly asked his six-year-old daughter.

"No, I guess I'm not much good," the little girl replied.

"Then," asked the father, "why do we keep you?"

"I suppose it is because mother loves me," was Joyce's solemn reply.

No philosopher or theologian could have given a better answer or spoken more truly. The real value that we place on anything is measured by the love we have for it.

I hold in my hand a Teddy bear (display) which certainly would not have much value in the market place of today. The fuzz has worn off its body; its ears have been chewed until they hang shapeless; one eye is gone, and the other has lost its animation. But I know a little girl to whom this Teddy bear has a value beyond price. A friend gave it to her when she was quite young. It cost only ninety-eight cents. It was a case of love at first sight. When she was old enough to talk the little girl called it "Bobo." Every night she went to sleep with "Bobo" in her arms. "Bobo" seemed to supply a need in her life.

When she was six years old her mother bought her an expensive big Teddy bear. But its cost and size meant nothing to the little girl, because her heart belonged to "Bobo," whose worth was measured only by her love for it. So does God measure our worth to Him—by His love for us.

I am now thinking of a little girl who was stricken with a severe case of poliomyelitis. She is now totally paralyzed. The doctors say that it is probable she will never walk again. She will be fortunate if she is ever able to feed herself. Her mother has to strap her in to keep her from falling out of her wheel chair. Unless a miracle happens she will never be able to do the things a normal person can do. It is probable that somebody will have to look after her as long as she lives, but her parents love her beyond measure.

In the Kentucky mountains a little girl was carrying her small crippled brother home on her back. As she paused at a mountain shack a neighbor said to her, "Put your burden down and come in and rest for a spell."

"I'll have you know," Ellen said, her eyes flashing, "that this ain't no burden I'm carrying. It's my little brother."

Carrying a brother whom we love is never a burden, because "love suffers long and is kind; love vaunteth not itself, is not puffed up." I think Jesus must have had some such thought in mind when He said, "Take my yoke upon you, and learn of me." In *Sidewalk Sermons* Dr. Roy Smith gives this striking illustration:

A beautifully gowned woman was out in the street, her arm bared to the elbow, as she searched in the mud and slime of the gutter for something. The crowd gathered and then came a policeman.

"What's the matter, lady? What are you hunting for?" the officer inquired, politely.

"I lost my ring," answered the woman, looking up, with big tears in her eyes. "It was a diamond ring that my husband gave me and I wouldn't lose it for the world. He was a soldier," she went on, sobbing now, "and he never came back. This ring was the only thing I had left that belonged to him."

This, then, was the explanation for the strange sight of a beautiful woman soiling her hands in the slime of a city gutter. Only a great love could have persuaded her to touch such filth.

It was love, too, that offered up the greatest sacrifice the world has ever seen. "For God so loved the world, that he gave his only begotten Son, that whosoever believeth in him should not perish, but have everlasting life." True love does not count the cost.

It is easy to know the genuine from the false by this simple test—true love seeks to give; false love seeks to get; true love asks, "How can I help?" False love asks, "What can I get?"

12. SATAN'S TRAPS

TEXT: *They lay wait, as he that setteth snares; they set a trap, they catch men.* JEREMIAH 5:26.

OBJECT: An ordinary steel trap which may be purchased at almost any hardware store.

THE LESSON: Here is a good strong steel trap which we shall use for the basis of our object lesson this morning. After we get the trap set (set the trap), we shall see if it works properly. (Insert a soft pine stick into the trap—one which has been previously prepared by cutting it almost in two so that the force of the trap will finish breaking it. Reset the trap.)

Now we know the trap will work. Which of you will come forward and stick your hand in it? What, no volunteers! Well, it looks as if I will have to put my hand in the steel trap. (There is really no trick to it. You simply thrust your fist into the trap and flip the trigger. Your fist is so large that the jaws will not have enough momentum to hurt you when they strike. Be sure to thrust your whole fist into the trap, not just a finger. If you are afraid to try it at first with your bare fist, put on a heavy glove.)

You see that it was possible for me to put my hand in the steel trap and not get hurt, but it is not possible for me or anyone else to play with Satan's traps without getting seriously hurt.

The prophet Jeremiah once said: "For among my people are found wicked men: they lay wait, as he that setteth snares; they set a trap, they catch men." Job complained, "The snare is laid for him in the ground." The writer of the Book of Ecclesiastes referred to the perils thus: "As the fishes that are taken in an evil net, and as the birds that are caught in the snare; so are the sons of men snared in an evil time." The Psalmist knew well the reality of them and he prayed to be delivered from the pestilence that walketh in darkness and the destruction that wasteth at noonday.

Now let us take a look at some of the modern traps into which the feet of youth may fall.

1. There Are the Hidden Traps. When we set out to trap one kind of animal, we usually conceal the trap so that the animal will not be able to see it. Then when the animal steps on the trigger of the trap its powerful jaws close on the animal's feet, and it is trapped. For another kind of animal we bait the trap

with a piece of meat or something else in order to lure the animal into the trap.

Today Satan has all kinds of traps set for our feet. Some of Satan's traps are cleverly concealed so that we may walk into them unaware. Others are baited with something that appeals to our appetite. The trap of alcoholism is carefully hidden among surroundings of respectability and decency. Our radios and television constantly sing praise of alcoholic beverages, and advertisements in newspapers and magazines try to convince us that men and women of distinction consider the drinking of hard liquor as good form. A social drink or a bottle of beer seems so harmless that we do not see the hidden trap which has been set for our feet.

Once I was asked to visit a prisoner who had been condemned to die in the electric chair for the murder of his wife. For more than an hour I sat with him in his cell and listened to his story of the tragic events which had led to his crime and pending punishment.

"I did love my wife," he said, "and I never would have killed her if I had not been drunk and crazy at the time. When I took my first drink I did not think that I would keep on drinking until I had lost all self-respect and self-control."

Sometimes we step into one of Satan's concealed traps, or we may be lured into a trap which has been carefully baited to appeal to our appetite. We must ever be on the alert for these traps.

2. The Trap of Popularity. This is a very dangerous trap because of the very nature of boys and girls.

The strongest human desire is the desire to be loved. Anything which helps us in our efforts to win the approval of our friends serves like a tonic for us. Many of our social customs and current practices are centered around the idea of winning the approval of our friends. Girls wear lipstick and paint their fingernails red because they have learned that some boys like that kind of thing. Boys get crew haircuts and wear red neckties because experience has taught them that some girls like such haircuts and ties. One of the most difficult things a boy or girl has to do is to swim against the tide of public opinion. Anything which is highly popular is almost certain to be worldly in nature. Jesus pointed out that straight is the way and narrow is the gate that leads to eternal life, and few there be that find it. On the other hand, the road that leads to destruction is a broad highway and many there be who will go in thereat.

When everybody begins to love you, make much over you, and say a few nice things about you, it is getting time to start looking for a hidden trap of one kind or another. We must remember that Christianity never has been, nor ever can be, an easy-going religion. That is true because Christianity calls on men and women to forget themselves and to make sacrifices for the Kingdom of God. Anything that requires a real sacrifice does not come very easily.

3. The Trap of Indifference. Indifference means unconcern or just a lack of interest. Many boys and girls who will openly tell you that they do not pretend to be religious will not go so far as to say that they

are actually irreligious. They believe they are neutral. They are not going to bother with religion and they don't want religion to bother them. Each year there are thousands of young people who fall into the trap of indifference. It begins in a very harmless way. There is a football game Saturday night or a party or other form of entertainment, which goes on until the wee hours of the morning, and when Sunday morning arrives there is just no desire to get up and go to church. If a person has attended Sunday school irregularly for a number of months he begins to lose interest altogether. And as he does so, he frequently tells himself that the church is all wrong. When he begins to look for faults in the church and among the people who constitute the church he is certain to find them.

So, finally, he decides that he will do nothing about religion, either to oppose or to promote it. He will be indifferent—or neutral. But we cannot be neutral toward religion. A man cannot say that he will have neither weeds nor roses in his garden. He may have roses if he will plant them and cultivate them, but if he will not plant and cultivate them, nature will step in and decide the matter for him: he will have weeds, whether he wants them or not. The same principle applies in the area of religion. If we want to follow Christian ideals, we can do so if we are willing to make the effort through prayer and practice. But if we do not, then Satan will decide the matter for us. He will step in and fill our lives with all kinds of evil things, whether we like it or not. So we need be constantly on guard against the traps that Satan sets for us, especially the trap of popularity and the trap of indifference.

13. SHAKE WELL

TEXT: *Wherefore I put thee in remembrance, that thou stir up the gift of God, which is in thee by the putting on of my hands.* II TIMOTHY 1:6.

OBJECTS: A bottle of medicine which must be shaken before it is used.

THE LESSON: I hold a bottle of medicine in my hand. On the label I read these words, "Shake well before using." I look at the bottle carefully and notice dark sediment at the bottom and clear liquid above. I shake the bottle, and now the contents are well mixed and ready for use.

This bottle of medicine may well serve as an example of the way some of us treat our religion. We may have in our minds and hearts some of the basic teachings of Jesus, but we permit these great truths to settle down to the bottom of our lives and do not use them. Paul once wrote to his young friend Timothy and advised him to stir up the gift of God that was within him. Evidently young Timothy had permitted his religion to become separated from his daily life. Paul wanted Timothy to stir his gifts up so that there would be power and purpose in his life. The man who had only one talent and did not use it failed to stir up the gift of God that was in him. God has given us the gifts that we possess, and He requires us to use them rightly. If we fail to use them, they will eventually become atrophied.

If we are to stir up the gift of God that is within us we must know what that gift is. Sometimes we may try to stir up a gift which we do not possess. When I was a boy I wanted to learn to pick a five-string banjo. I spent several years trying to pick a banjo before discovering that though I had the desire I did not have the gift.

Each young person should discover what his talents are and pray that the Lord will direct him to use them to the best purpose. God will show us our place in life if we will earnestly seek His guidance. I believe that with all of my heart. When God leads us into a trade or into a profession, we will never stand among the failures. Someone has said that there are too many square people in round holes and too many round people in square holes, and there is much truth in that observation. But if you will pray for God to lead you, He will hear and answer your prayers.

Let us take a look at a few of the precious gifts which are so vitally needed in the work of the church today.

The first one that comes to mind is the ability to promote peace and harmony among people. Sometimes a misunderstanding will arise in a young people's meeting that will create tension. Then some level-headed person who has the gift will pour oil on the troubled waters by offering a suggestion that will ease the tension and bring harmony to the group. Blessed is the peacemaker who uses his talent to promote the Kingdom of God.

Then there is the person with the gift for caring. He loves his Lord and his church, and he wants to see their influence grow. He cares about every phase of the work of the church. He prays for his church, works for it, gives to it. He cares enough to be at its services every time the door is open.

Another may be possessed with the spirit of optimism. May the Lord bless him and his kind. No matter how blue and discouraging the future may look, it is never hopeless so long as there are a few Josiahs and Calebs who believe that with God's help the job can be done. All the great characters of the Bible were gifted with a dauntless spirit. Blessed are those who have the gift of optimism. They get stirred up for the glory of God. They are among the chief supporters of the church.

The last gift we shall mention is the gift of enthusiasm. I recently attended a news conference at which the Rev. Billy Graham was the principal speaker. At the close of the service he invited all who would like to have a deeper religious experience to meet him in a large assembly room after the benediction had been pronounced. No pressure of any kind was brought to bear on the audience. More than five hundred young people responded to the invitation. After the meeting was over, I overheard a high-school senior say to his girl friend, "Billy Graham is bubbling over with enthusiasm. He makes a fellow want to search for the best that is in his soul."

"But," replied the girl friend, "the best cannot get into one's soul until one lets Jesus come in."

If we will stir up the gift of God that is within us, we will always find room for more of the love and guidance of our Saviour.

14. HALF-BAKED BOYS AND GIRLS

TEXT: *Beloved, think it not strange concerning the fiery trial which is to try you, as though some strange thing happened unto you.* I PETER 4:12.

OBJECTS: A few grains of wheat, a glass of water, some yeast, and a piece of bread.

THE LESSON: If I were to tell you that the same method has to be followed in making a good boy or girl as is followed in making a good loaf of bread you would probably laugh at the idea. And yet it is true. We have here four things which go into the making of a loaf of bread.

1. Wheat. The wheat is the substance of which bread is made. So before we can get the bread, the wheat has to be ground to get the flour out of it. Our word "bread" comes from the word which means to pound or to crush. This old word is "brayed." Bread comes from brayed wheat, so we shorten the word and call it bread.

Most boys and girls have to be brayed or whipped before they are fit for use. So when your parents whip you they don't do it just to make your life more miserable. When my father used to tell me that whipping me would hurt him more than it did me I did not believe it. Now, since I have a child of my own, I have a deep understanding of just what he meant. When your parents punish you they are trying to help you get rid of your undesirable qualities, just as the farmer has to bray his wheat to get rid of the husk. And so, like wheat, a child has to be brayed or whipped occasionally. Solomon warned the parents of his day against the danger of sparing the rod and spoiling the child.

2. Water. In order to make bread the flour must be moistened. This word "moisten" reminds us of the hard work we must do before we can amount to very much. When God drove Adam and Eve from the Garden of Eden He told them that they would have to earn their bread by the sweat of their brows. That means that they would have to work for their bread. The boy or girl who is always trying to dodge work seldom amounts to very much. Paul once told a group of men that if they would not work they could not eat. As you can't make bread without moistening the flour, so you can't make fine men and women out of boys and girls who are not willing to earn their living by the sweat of their brows.

3. Yeast. The next thing that goes into a good loaf of bread is yeast. The yeast causes the dough to rise.

Without yeast the dough would bake into such a hard lump that it could not be easily digested.

Now, God's Word works in the life of boys and girls as yeast works in dough. It gives them the inspiration they need to make them sing as they work. The Bible says that those who trust God will be so happy and light-hearted that they shall mount up on the wings like eagles—they shall run and not be weary. The Word of God is the great yeast that lightens labor and puts life into your work. While yeast is a silent agent, it is also a very active agent. Put a small lump of yeast into a large lump of dough and the whole lump will be leavened. Jesus said that the Kingdom of God is like yeast. We simply cannot have Christianity and keep it to ourselves. If we have it at all we just have to give it away.

4. Baking. As we behold this piece of bread we know that it has gone through the process of baking. It takes a hot fire to make loaves of bread.

One of the apostles said, "Think it not strange concerning the fiery trial which is to try you." He meant that every strong character has to be tested by the fire of temptation. One of the writers of the Old Testament said that Ephraim was like a half-baked fig. He meant that Ephraim had not been hardened. When we say that a boy is only half-baked we mean that he is soft and pliable like dough. Every time you overcome a temptation you are being made into a more wholesome boy or girl. Put your trust in God; He will help you come safely through the fiery furnace of temptation.

Because of His love for a lost humanity, Jesus was willing to be misunderstood, misrepresented, slandered, ridiculed, and finally crucified.

Man's worth is measured by the price God was willing to pay for his rescue. What we are capable of being may be guessed by the efforts Jesus made to free us from sin.

You boys and girls may not be much good to your parents, but I am sure that they want to keep you because they love you. God loves you not so much for what you are today as for what you are capable of becoming if only you will accept His saving grace and let Him come and live in your heart.

15. FIDDLING AROUND

TEXT: *So likewise, whosoever he be of you that forsaketh not all that he hath, he cannot be my disciple.* LUKE 14:33.

OBJECTS: A violin with three large cardboard tags tied to it.

THE LESSON: I hold in my hands a musical instrument which has at least two names. When it is played in the rural areas of America or in connection with ballads or hill-billy tunes, it is usually called a fiddle. But when it is played in connection with opera or classical music it is called a violin.

The violin was invented in the thirteenth century

and reached its highest degree of perfection about four hundred years later in the hands of Antonius Stradivarius. First and foremost among the violin makers were those living in the little Italian city of Cremona. There the Amati family produced many fine instruments, which became known as fiddles. When someone asked Stradivarius to explain the difference between the violin and the fiddle he is reported to have replied, "The fiddle becomes a violin only when it is in the hands of an artist."

Since I do not have the hands of an artist, I will be quite literal and call this instrument a fiddle. You will notice that there are three tags tied to this fiddle and that each tag has something written on it which describes a way in which the fiddle can be played. Let's take a look at these tags and see what they say. (Remove first tag and read.)

1. Fiddling Around. That is the way many people spend their precious time—just fiddling around. Such fiddling is most often done by boys and girls shopping around in an effort to find something which will capture their interest and their loyalty. Instead of buckling down and doing their own work they just fiddle around listening to the radio, watching television, or dreaming of the years which lie ahead.

Quite often the habits of fiddling around persist into the teens and adulthood. Many boys and girls grow up like the boy described by Riley Scott in "Just Hanging Around," even though they may not come to such a tragic end:

I met him first when he was just a little lad,
And I asked, "Whither bound?"
And the answer that he gave me made me feel quite
    sad,
For he said, "I am hanging, just hanging around."

When I saw him next he was tall with youth,
But no new traits I found,
For he was still hanging, just hanging around.

When I saw him again he was a full-grown man,
But he had not changed his life-long plan,
For he was still hanging, just hanging around.

Then one day I saw the hangman fix the noose
    about his neck,
And lift him some ten feet off the ground,
And I left him hanging—just hanging around.

You cannot read the Bible long without coming to
the conclusion that we who are made in the image of
God were created for a purpose. Think of Abraham
going out and not knowing whither he went, of Daniel
walking into a den of lions rather than surrender his
faith in God, of the Apostle Paul living with a noble
purpose and dying not in vain—and we can see that
such men were instruments through which God works.
Christ moved through Galilee calling to men, saying,
"Follow me." All through history men and women
have answered that call and have found that God gives
power and purpose to life.

If you boys and girls want to be somebody tomor-
row, you must begin to be somebody today. When Jesus was twelve years old He said that He had to be

about His Father's business. Let us now look at the second tag and see what is on it.

2. Playing Second Fiddle. We are all more or less familiar with the phrase, "playing second fiddle." It is a figure of speech which means that we are taking second place. No girl likes to play second fiddle to a girl who always gets the best dates while she takes what is left. No red-blooded boy likes to play on the scrub team if he is qualified to make the first team.

We live in a world which limits itself to second-rate interests. Amusements and worldly pleasures demand so much of youth's time that it is often quite difficult to find a moment to sit down and think seriously about the most satisfying and most rewarding things in life.

So because we do not know the great and abiding things which belong to eternity we control ourselves with the second-rate things of the world. God demands our first loyalty and interest, and we must give Him our best or nothing. Now let's look at the third tag and see what it says.

3. Fiddling While Rome Burns. We know that Nero did not fiddle while Rome burned, for the fiddle had not been invented at that time. However, the saying, "fiddling while Rome burns," has come to mean engagement in foolish things while danger and destruction are all around us.

Today our world is on fire. The threat of war continues to hang over us. People everywhere hurry hither and yon looking for something to ease their nerves and lessen their tension. They flock to places of entertainment and pour their wealth into liquor, tobacco, sleeping pills and sedatives in a desperate effort to find some sort of lasting peace. They neglect their private devotions, public worship, and their duties to God. Millions of people today feel no sense of stewardship whatsoever, no strong desire to travel the high road of life, no conscious need of God. I beg you to get rid of these silly habits and take Jesus Christ as your Lord and Saviour. He is waiting now to receive you with open arms.

16. A SPANKING GOOD PIECE

TEXT: *And Paul, earnestly beholding the council, said, Men and brethren, I have lived in all good conscience before God until this day.* ACTS 23:1.

OBJECT: The heart of a ripe watermelon.

THE LESSON: We have here a heart of a nice, ripe watermelon which reminds me of my childhood days on a farm. When we began to eat a watermelon we would cut a nice piece out of the center of the melon so that we would have a choice piece on which to quit. It was commonly called the "spanky piece." That "spanky piece" would leave a good taste in our mouths. Saving the best until the last is a custom widely practiced among boys and girls. We like to save our dessert until last because we know that it will leave a good taste in our mouths. I know a little girl who wants to hold on to a certain comic-paper strip until the last because she considers it the best. And so she holds it back and waits until she has read all the others.

One of the wise men of the Bible expressed that philosophy in his description of the times and seasons. He went on to say that there is a time to be born and a time to die, a time to sing and a time to dance, a time to embrace and a time to refrain from embracing. He goes on with the description of the times and seasons until he finally brings out the last and the best. The best part of life should always be ahead of you and not behind you. Sometimes we hear old people say, "If only I could call back ten, fifteen, or twenty years, I would do such and such a thing." Well, that may be true for many old people, but it should not be true even when people grow old.

The Apostle Peter said that we should grow in grace and in knowledge of our Lord and Saviour, Jesus Christ. As you boys and girls grow physically and mentally, you should also grow in grace. As you learn more about the principles of Jesus, the more Christ-like you should become.

During the Christmas holidays a famous Kentucky woman and her husband entered one of the fashion-able eating establishments of Nashville. The place was crowded and the only available seats were at a table occupied by two well-dressed young people who proved to be very congenial. But a few minutes after the Kentucky couple had left the table the woman dis-covered that she had left her purse containing a large amount of money and other valuables lying on the table. She sought in vain to find the only two people who might have found her purse. A few days later she made an appeal over the radio in which she said, "If the finder of my purse will please send me the little pencil that was in the purse he may have the purse and all that it contains. The actual value of the pencil is almost nothing, but it means a lot to me. It was given to me by my little crippled daughter, who is now dead. When she gave it to me she said, 'Mommy, I want you to keep this pencil always. If anything should happen to me I want you to keep this pencil and remember that I will be waiting for you in Paradise.'"

At last account, the woman had not found her precious pencil, but she still had a heart-warming memory of her daughter and a fond hope to which she could cling.

Some of you will perhaps remember Sidney Carton, the jackal, in *The Tale of Two Cities*. Sidney was a self-centered personality who thought only of himself. Whatever he did, his motives were selfish. But one day he slipped into a prison cell and there he forgot himself. He took another man's place at the guillotine, and those who saw him die said that his face was the most peaceful on which they had ever looked. They were all convinced that Sidney had saved the best part of his personality until the last critical hour.

Paul lived a hard and rugged life. At last he was condemned to die and then while he was waiting in the death cell for the last hour to pass, he said, "I have lived in all good conscience before God. I have kept the faith. I have finished the course. I know that there is a crown of righteousness laid up for me." What a "spanking" good piece of philosophy to hold onto when everything else has failed! Now the Lord teaches us that there is always something better for the Christian, and He described heaven as a beautiful place not built with hands but with eternal love—a place where there will be no more sickness or sorrow, or pain, or crying, or death, for all of the former things will have passed away. So, no matter what happens to us, we can always hold on to the very best until the last. Then we can enjoy it as a part of our inheritance in the Kingdom of God prepared for us from the foundation of the world. Every Christian can truly say, "The best is yet to come."

17. THROWING MONKEY WRENCHES

TEXT: *For God so loved the world, that he gave his only begotten Son, that whosoever believeth in him should not perish, but have everlasting life.* JOHN 3:16.

OBJECT: A monkey wrench.

THE LESSON: A high school senior was the center of attraction while she poured out her heart to her classmates. The other girls listened to her with a great deal of interest, for they understood her language and sympathized with her predicament. She was telling the other girls how she had her boy friend securely tied to her apron strings until a new girl came on the scene. And then the new girl threw a monkey wrench into her plans.

They all understood what it means for a girl to have a monkey wrench thrown into her plans, but I doubt that many of them understood how that slang expression came into being.

Throwing a monkey wrench is a slang expression that came into use a good many years ago in the huge wheat fields of the West. Once, in the midst of the harvest season, a series of misunderstandings arose between the harvesters and the owners of the wheat fields. A few of the more belligerent harvesters decided to get even with their employers by concealing steel monkey wrenches in the sheaves of wheat. When the sheaves were fed into the threshing machine the monkey wrenches concealed in them wrecked the machines. Sometimes sparks caused by steel clashing on steel would start a fire and much wheat would be burned. In some sections of the wheat belt the saboteurs did so much damage with their monkey wrenches that whole crops of wheat were destroyed.

To throw a monkey wrench into machinery has come to mean almost any effort designed to block or to hinder somebody's plans. Now, there are many ways of throwing monkey wrenches into machinery and many kinds of people who throw them, but it is our purpose to discuss those who throw monkey wrenches into the circle of the church and its organization.

The Apostle Paul was well acquainted with monkey-wrench throwers. People were always throwing monkey wrenches into his plans, but he kept right on preaching the gospel.

The third Epistle of John is a very interesting letter of only fourteen verses. The author is reminding his friend that there is a monkey-wrench thrower in their midst. His name is Diotrephes and he is evidently a man of great influence.

"I wrote unto the church:" says John, "but Diotrephes, who loveth to have the pre-eminence among them, receiveth us not. Wherefore, if I come, I will remember his deeds which he doeth, prating against us with malicious words: and not content therewith, neither doth he himself receive the brethren, and forbiddeth them that would, and casteth them out of the church" (III John 9 and 10).

The spirit of Diotrephes still lives. That spirit is often seen by those who work with boys and girls in our own church.

One of the most tragic things about people who throw monkey wrenches into the machinery of a church organization is that often they do it with the best of motives. They may sincerely feel that if only they can stop a movement with which they do not agree they will be rendering a great service to the Kingdom of God. They fail to see that their monkey wrenches might do much more harm than would the movement to which they are so opposed.

Jesus Christ made it crystal clear that the Kingdom of God cannot be promoted simply by trying to enforce a set of rules, no matter how fine the rules may be. You boys and girls cannot promote the spirit of

Jesus in your Sunday-school class by simply forcing a bad boy to stop chewing bubble gum while the teacher is leading a prayer. The bad boy is not likely to be very deeply impressed by goodness that is negative.

I am now thinking of a boy who quit singing in the Junior Choir because he did not like the boisterous conduct of some of the other members of the choir. He took his grievance to his father, who, in turn, made an issue out of it to the official board of the church. After a sharp disagreement took place among the officers of the church, the choir director resigned and the Junior Choir broke up. Now the church does not have a Junior Choir and most of the juniors do not even remain for the Sunday morning service. The monkey wrench thrown by the boy did much more harm than good. If he had worked patiently from the inside he might have succeeded in changing the situation to which he objected. He gained his point, but he lost his opportunity in the process. He thought he had won, but really he had lost.

There is an old Chinese proverb that says, "It is foolish to burn down the barn to get rid of the rats." It is equally foolish to throw a monkey wrench into some church movement or project with which we do not wholly agree in order to have our way. The next time you feel like throwing a monkey wrench at something, think twice—and then don't throw it.

18. GIVE ME YOUR HEART

TEXT: *Trust in the Lord with all thine heart; and lean not unto thine own understanding.* PROVERBS 3:5.

OBJECT: A small heart-shaped candy box. Paint the box red and place in it twelve small cards, with one of the following words written on each card: jealousy, dishonesty, untruthfulness, hate, greed, unforgiveness, love, forgiveness, generosity, loyalty, faith, and hope. If it is not convenient to get such a box, a small cardboard heart painted red on one side, with the above words written on the other side will suffice. Conceal the box underneath the coat of a boy who has agreed to advance to help with the experiment. Have him come to the platform as you begin.

THE LESSON: Johnny has agreed to assist us with our demonstration this morning and we shall begin by asking him this simple question, "Johnny, what have you in your heart?" (He will probably say that he doesn't know, or smile and say nothing.) "Well, since you do not seem quite certain what you do have in your heart, let us begin a little investigation to see if we can discover what you have in it." (Slip your hand under the boy's coat and, after a show of effort, bring out the heart.)

(Open the box and take the card with the word JEALOUSY written on it.) "Oh, I see that you have jealousy in your heart. Now, jealousy is a very dangerous sin. It will cause a boy to think mean and ugly thoughts about anyone who threatens to outshine him. If a boy permits jealousy to remain in his heart it will breed envy and mistrust and he will soon be trying to discredit anyone who threatens his place in the sun. Unless he removes the jealousy from his heart it will eventually destroy him."

As you pick up the cards which contain the words (dishonesty, hate, untruthfulness, greed, unforgiveness) show how each is the product of sin. Then take the other six cards which contain the words (love, forgiveness, loyalty, generosity, faith, hope), and show how each is a product of Christianity.

Now let's look at some reasons why you should give your heart to Jesus.

1. It Is the Right Thing To Do. God created you in His own image and He gave you life. Your life has to be spent. Physical death does not end life. The bad as well as the good live on after death. The bad or the sinful spend eternity in hell. The good or the redeemed spend eternity in heaven. Heaven is a place of joy. Hell is a place of torment. You should give your heart to Jesus because it is the right thing to do.

2. It Is to Your Interest To Give Your Heart to Jesus. Your heart, as Jesus thought and spoke of the heart, is your most precious possession. When Jesus

spoke of the heart He usually meant that part of our nature that loves and trusts and obeys. That is what Jesus is asking when He says, "Give me thine heart," or, in other words, "Give me your love, your talents, your ambitions, your desires." It is to your interest to give your heart to Jesus. When your heart is in His keeping then you are safe.

3. You Will Enjoy Doing It. After you have given your heart to Jesus you will know a special kind of happiness which is unknown to the unsaved. You will know that God is your Father and that you are His beloved child. You will know that your heavenly Father loves you and will provide the very best for you both here and hereafter. When God lives in your heart you will have love and happiness. Outside circumstances cannot rob you of that happiness. Some people have the mistaken idea that to give their hearts to Jesus will be to live in a state of gloom forever. But the facts are that the happiest and most enthusiastic people in the world are Christian people. There is a big difference between fun and happiness. Fun may be created from the outside, but happiness is always born from within.

There can be no real happiness in a heart filled with sin and guilt and shame. But when we let Jesus come into our hearts He forgives us our sins and fills our hearts with peace and joy.

I beg you to commit your hearts to Jesus, who alone can satisfy your deepest desires and make you feel that you are a child of a Saviour who cares.

"Trust in the Lord with all thine heart; and lean

not unto thine own understanding" (Proverbs 3:5).

"For the eyes of the Lord run to and fro through the whole earth, to shew himself strong in the behalf of them whose heart is perfect toward Him" (II Chronicles 16:9).

19. BIG BUGS

TEXT: *But ye shall receive power, after that the Holy Ghost is come upon you.* ACTS 1:8.

OBJECTS: Several snapping or boring beetles in a big glass jar. These beetles may be found in almost any old rotten tree trunk.

THE LESSON: Some time ago a modern young woman called the church office and wanted to speak to one of the "big bugs" of the church. I told her that I was not a very big bug but might be able to give her the information she wanted. Later I turned to *Webster's Dictionary* and found that the expression "big bug" or "big shot" was a term used to describe a pompous or pretentious person.

We have here in this jar some big bugs, called snapping or boring beetles. They have powerful pincers, which enable them to dominate the smaller bugs with which they come in contact.

When we say that a person is a "big bug" or "big shot," we usually mean that he is someone who possesses means by which he gets people to do the things he wants done.

Every age has its own standard for judging bigness. There was a time when the big man was the person who could hit the hardest with his fist or shoot the straightest with his gun. But that type of bigness was gradually pushed into the background by men who could outthink their opponents, men who could hire other men to do their fighting for them. Then came the age when great scholars became the "big men" of their day. Great men like Martin Luther, John Calvin, and John Wesley became the most powerful men in the world.

But today, in the thinking of many, the "big man" is the boss, the man who writes the checks, the man who inspects the job, or the man who hires and fires. For you boys and girls the big man may be your high-school principal or your father, for we all have to recognize someone who holds authority over us.

Paul once wrote a letter to the "big men" of Colossae in which he reminded them that God was bigger than any living man, that while the big men had authority over the men who worked for them, God had authority over everyone.

Jesus once reminded His disciples that a big person was not one who wielded the greatest authority over others, but one who was most willing to serve others. That is what He meant when He said, "For whosoever will save his life shall lose it; but whosoever shall lose his life for my sake and the gospel's, the same shall save it." When the disciples met with Jesus in the upper room, they all had ideas of being "big men," but they misunderstood the meaning of bigness. It was an Oriental custom for servants to dust the feet of the guests on arrival. But on this occasion no servant was present, and no one wanted to do a servant's job. Then Jesus took a towel and stooped down and washed the feet of the disciples. In doing that He taught them the real meaning of bigness.

The biggest boy or the biggest girl in this group may not be the tallest or the one who weighs the most, but the one who tries the hardest to be a close follower of Jesus Christ. In this sense you will be big boys and girls. If you follow Jesus, you can all be big boys and girls.

Zaccheus was a little man, and he had to climb a tree to get a better view of Jesus as He passed by. But Zaccheus was not little at heart, for when he accepted Jesus as his Saviour he became one of the biggest men in his community. So you and I may become big personalities if we will let the Spirit of God live in our hearts.

And that brings us to five important requirements for being a Christian.

1. You must believe in Jesus Christ. "For God so loved the world, that he gave his only begotten Son, that whosoever believeth in him should not perish, but have everlasting life" (John 3:16).

"He that believeth on him is not condemned: but he that believeth not is condemned already, because he hath not believed in the name of the only begotten Son of God" (John 3: 18).

2. You must repent. "Repent ye therefore, and be converted, that your sins may be blotted out" (Acts 3:19). To repent is to be sorry for your sins and try not to sin any more.

3. You must accept Jesus not only as your Saviour but also as your Lord and Master. When we accept Jesus as our Saviour, we may be thinking of getting something from Him; but when we accept Him as our Lord and Master we are usually thinking in terms of what we can do for the Kingdom of God.

4. Jesus invites you to accept Him. "Come unto me, all ye that labour and are heavy laden, and I will give you rest" (Matthew 11:28).

"Suffer little children and forbid them not to come unto me: for of such is the kingdom of heaven." (Matthew 19:14).

5. Jesus promises to receive you. "All that the Father giveth me shall come to me; and him that cometh to me I will in no wise cast out" (John 6:37).

If you will do these things, then, not only will you grow in grace and in knowledge of our Lord and Saviour Jesus Christ but you will become big in the eyes of God.

20. TALKING THROUGH YOUR HAT

TEXT: *When thou shalt vow a vow unto the Lord thy God, thou shalt not slack to pay it.* DEUTERONOMY 23:21.

OBJECTS: A hat and a pair of large scissors. Cut the crown out of the hat just before you begin and talk to your audience through the hole in your hat. The better the hat, the more impressive your lesson will be.

THE LESSON: Once, while talking with a group of carefree youngsters who were waiting for a bus, I became interested in a conversation between two fellow passengers who were evidently on their way home from school. The boy was trying to win an exclusive place in the affections of his girl friend, and was making some very fair promises to her. He told her that if she would "go steady" with him that he would never so much as look at another girl and that he would not go out at night any more without her permission and would work hard and try to raise his grades above the "C" level. Her reply to his fair promises was, "Oh, you're just talking through your hat."

In modern slang, to talk through your hat means to say things you do not mean or to make promises you have no intention of keeping. Sometimes people make promises in good faith and later find they are unable to keep them. One day in 1929 a millionaire real estate operator came to the college campus where I was a student and promised to give the college a million-dollar football stadium. Classes were suspended for the day and the students were delighted. Three weeks later the stock market crashed and the millionaire became a pauper almost overnight.

If you make a promise to God and are unable to keep your promise He has the power to release you from your obligations.

Today is Rally Day in our Church and it also marks the beginning of our Loyalty Campaign, which will run for thirteen weeks. Most of you boys and girls have promised to be present every Sunday for the next thirteen Sundays and I know that you were not just talking through your hat when you made those promises.

Now let us have a concrete example of what it means to talk through your hat. (Cut the crown out of the hat and then talk through the crown to the audience.) If you boys and girls will be present every Sunday for the next thirteen Sundays, I will guarantee that each of you will make high grades at school and that you will not have a single care or disappointment during that period, and at the end of this Loyalty Campaign I will give each boy and each girl a brand-new one-hundred-dollar bill as a bonus. (Lay the hat aside.)

These promises may sound attractive to some of you, but you must remember that I was talking through my hat and have no intention of ever trying to fulfill any of them.

In the fourth chapter of the Book of Matthew we have a good example of how the devil tried to tempt Jesus with promises he could not keep. "Again, the devil taketh him up into an exceeding high mountain, and sheweth him all of the kingdoms of the world, and the glory of them; and said unto him, All these things will I give thee, if thou wilt fall down and worship me." The devil was talking through his hat. He was offering kingdoms which were not his to give.

The devil is still talking through his hat. He is still offering to boys and girls many prizes and bonuses which they will never get. He offers you tricks and dishonesty as a means by which you can make good grades in school. He is still offering you all kinds of attractive propositions, but he has no intention of keeping his promises.

On one occasion Peter told Jesus that he would be faithful to Him at all costs, but a few hours later he was denying that he had ever known Jesus.

When I go over the church roll I find hundreds of members who once stood here at the altar and promised before high heaven that they would be loyal to their church and to their God, but who are now listed among the unfaithful. They were talking through their hats.

Some men who win an official place in a church and promise to be loyal officers do not keep their promises and we discover that they were talking through their hats.

May God help us to keep the promises we make. And may we also remember that we can read the promises of God and know that they will be kept. When Jesus said, "I will give unto you the keys of the kingdom of heaven," He was speaking a truth which has been verified by generations since. God will keep His promises to you, so try to keep your promises to Him.

21. TO GIVE THE GATE

TEXT: *If ye abide in me, and my words abide in you, ye shall ask what ye will, and it shall be done unto you.* JOHN 15:7.

OBJECT: A small wooden gate made of sticks or lattice.

THE LESSON: We have here a little wooden gate around which we shall build our object lesson for this morning. The idea for this lesson came to me last week after I had accidentally overheard a conversation between a group of high-school girls sitting in a drugstore and discussing some of their many social problems.

One of the girls did most of the talking. She was telling her friends about her ex-boy friend.

"He stood me up twice," she said, with a toss of her pretty head, "so when he came last night I gave him the gate. He took the gate right off the bat and then he took a powder."

At first I wondered what did happen to the poor boy, but after I got home and consulted my dictionary on slang I discovered that his predicament might not have been as bad as at first I had feared.

"To give the gate" means, in modern slang, to put an end to a friendly relationship or abruptly to dismiss an idea or a person from one's mind or presence.

In the tenth chapter of Mark we discover a very promising young man who, after discussing his problem with Jesus, decides that he will give Jesus the gate. The first time we see this young man he is running toward Jesus. His heart is beating fast and his hopes are running high. A crowd has gathered on the coast of Judea to greet Jesus. Parents are bringing their children to Jesus in order that He may bless them. But this eager young man pushes past the crowd and runs to meet Jesus.

He is known as the rich young ruler. At first he runs to Jesus, but after the interview we see him walking away sorrowfully. Now, this sort of thing is happening all the time. We rush up to something, read the price tag on it, decide that we are not willing to pay the price, and then walk away with great sadness in our hearts.

Boys and girls are still rushing up to things and then walking away sorrowfully. A young person wants to be a great singer so he rushes up to music. But when he realizes that it will take years of patient work and self discipline to become a good singer he gives the idea the gate and walks away with sadness in his heart. Or may be he will run up and say, "I want to be an author," but when he sees that the price tag calls for toil, patience, and long years of practice, he gives the idea the gate and walks away sorrowfully.

I am now thinking of a young man who was a candidate for the ministry. While in the seminary he met and fell in love with a girl who did not believe in Jesus Christ. The young man soon decided that he would have to choose between the ministry and the girl he loved. She told him frankly that she could never marry him unless he was willing to give up the ministry. Being very much in love with the girl, he gave Jesus the gate and married the girl. The marriage ended in failure.

Fortunately, not all boys and girls have to choose between Jesus and the person they love the most. But we all do have to choose between good and evil and we might well remember that the Christian way is the only way which will lead us to the worth-while goals in life. Blessed is he who runs up to Jesus, accepts Him, and then walks with Him all the way.

So we see the young man of the Bible running up to Jesus, but walking away sorrowfully. Just what did the young man want when he came to Jesus? He wanted exactly what you want, what I want, and what every member of this congregation wants. He wanted eternal life. The idea of growing old and dying did not appeal to him any more than it appeals to us. Let him put it in his own words. "Good Master, what shall I do to inherit eternal life?"

The young man started out on the wrong track. It is quite probable that he had inherited his fortune and was thinking that he could inherit salvation in the same way. You boys and girls may inherit the possessions of your parents, but you cannot inherit their faith in God, their loyalty to the church or their salvation. Salvation is not something we may earn by our good works. It is not something which may be passed on to us from our parents. It is a gift of God. And this gift of God is bestowed only on those willing to pay the price. The young man wanted eternal life, but he was not willing to pay the price. Jesus told him that he would have to sell his property and give to the poor. The young man walked away sorrowfully, and we never hear of him again.

We can force a man to pay his taxes, but we cannot force him to be generous, because generosity is a condition of the heart. God gives us freedom of will and choice because He loves us. Character is achieved only by making decisions and reaching conclusions. I offer you Jesus Christ, the Son of God, and the Saviour of the world. Accept Him today.

22. GOD AND MAN

TEXT: *I am the vine, ye are the branches. He that abideth in me, and I in him, the same bringeth forth much fruit; for without me ye can do nothing.* JOHN 15:5.

OBJECTS: A pair of scissors and a screwdriver. Before beginning the lesson take the scissors apart and display the two single blades.

THE LESSON: We have here two single blades of a pair of scissors and a small metal screw which was made to hold the blades together. Without the tiny screw to hold these blades together they would be useless. I cannot imagine anything that one might well do with a single scissors blade. I might hold them together with my left hand while I attempt to use them with my right hand (demonstrate) but as soon as my left hand is removed the blades are again useless. But when I insert the screw in its proper place and tighten it the scissors are again ready for use.

The blades of these scissors might well represent the relationship between God and man, and the screw which holds them together and makes them serviceable might well represent the principles of Jesus as they are proclaimed in the New Testament. When man tries to live without taking into consideration the principles of Jesus he certainly cannot exert any great influence which will extend to posterity. I think that Jesus must have had some such thought in mind when He said, "Without me ye can do nothing." Without Jesus we can do nothing which will be permanent or abiding.

On the other hand, God needs man. That does not mean that God is as dependent on us as we are on Him. Since man was created in the image of God, he is a creature of God and should co-operate with his Creator. When we say that man was created in the image of God we do not mean that God has a physical body. One of the questions in the Shorter Catechism is, "What is God like?" The answer is "God is a spirit and has not a body like man." We are made in the image of God in that we are free to think, to choose, to will, to love, to make decisions, and to reach conclusions. The lower animals do not have the ability to think or to reason or to make plans for the future.

A dog may be taught a lot of tricks, but you cannot teach a dog to dream about his past or to worry about his future. You never saw a dog develop an inferiority complex because he was forced to lead a dog's life. You never saw a monkey refuse to eat a banana because his girl friend had hurt his feelings. You never saw a horse balk and refuse to go forward because he had no social security number and was not eligible for an old-age pension. The lower animals do not care about the past or worry about the future. But man, who was made in the image of God, is a thinking and willing being. He may regret the past or fear the future.

God without man would be inconceivable. Think how dreary this old world would be if there were no men or women or boys or girls on it. It would seem that God would have to start all over again and create human beings before He would accomplish His purpose. The history of civilization is the story of how God has tried to reveal Himself to man and how man has misunderstood or repulsed God's efforts. Throughout the ages God tried to reveal Himself to man through dreams, visions, prophets, judges, kings, miracles, but still man did not understand His true nature. Then God decided to take the form of human flesh and come down to earth as a man so that the people could see for themselves what God is really like. Jesus, the babe of the manger, was God in the form of a human being. A few people believed in Jesus and accepted Him as the only begotten Son of God, but the masses spurned Him. It was not until after Jesus died on the cross and rose from the grave that people began to understand what God is really like.

In his thirty-three brief years on earch Jesus left in the hearts of His disciples a set of basic principles which are sufficient to bind man and God together in a bond that not even death can break.

This little screw may well represent these principles of Jesus. (Put scissors back together.) Now the scissors are useful. They can be used to perform the task they were designed to perform.

God and man must be bound together by the principles of Jesus. When Jesus said, "What God has joined together let no man put asunder," He was talking about the relationship between a man and his wife. But, like many others of Jesus' sayings, that statement set forth a basic principle which included many more things than marriage. There are many great things in life which belong together. Religion and church attendance is such a union. If our religion is real we will want to worship God in church. If we divorce religion from church attendance, then church attendance becomes just another routine duty. If we divorce church attendance from religion, the chances are that our religion will eventually lose its zeal. It will become self-centered and not Christ-centered.

You boys and girls were made in the image of God, who wants you to work with Him in His efforts to make the world a better place in which to live. God needs your talents and you need God's help and guidance. Accept Jesus Christ as your Saviour and let His principles of life unite you with the great power of God, who then will bless you, and keep you and make His face to shine on you so that His power may be manifest in you.

23. STICKS AND YARDSTICKS

TEXT: *But he that is greatest among you shall be your servant.* MATTHEW 23:11.

OBJECT: A yardstick.

THE LESSON: There are many different ways of measuring things and many different things used to measure with. Recently a little girl told me that the doctor had just been to see her ill mother and had taken her temperature. When I asked her how much temperature her mother had she replied, "I don't quite know, but I think the doctor said she had about a half a quart." Today we want to talk about just one of the many things people use for measuring things—the yardstick.

Someone has said that a preacher who thinks by the inch and preaches by the yard ought to be kicked out by the foot. I am not going to preach to you this morning by the yard but about the yardstick.

There are all kinds of standards for measuring things. Almost any one of you can name dozens of standards by which things are measured—inches yards, quarts, gallons, bushels, barrels, ounces, pounds, kilowatts, fathoms, minutes, hours, weeks, years—the list is almost endless.

Each of you boys and girls has a standard by which you measure your response to the problems with which you are faced. If your standard is based on the principles of Jesus then your response will always be wholesome and Christian. You will not have to debate with yourself whether you will be honest or dishonest, truthful or untruthful, co-operative or belligerent. Your Christian standards will help you to choose that which is Christlike.

Now let us look at a few of the standards by which many boys and girls are greatly influenced.

1. EVERYBODY ELSE IS DOING IT is a standard for some. Boys and girls like to get in and do things with the gang. When I tried to tell a ten-year-old boy that cheating on his history test was wrong he looked me straight in the eye and said, "But, doctor, you don't understand. Almost every other boy in my class did the same thing."

It does not follow that what everybody else is doing, or what you believe everybody else is doing, is necessarily right. Often the term "everybody" is seriously exaggerated. When I investigated the case of the cheating on the history examination I found that actually "everybody" consisted of only a few members of a single class.

2. IS IT THE POPULAR THING TO DO? is a standard by which many boys and girls decide their problems. A popular girl may go to school wearing a yellow ribbon in her hair and within a few days half the girls in her class may be wearing yellow ribbons in their hair. Now, there is certainly nothing wrong

about a girl wearing a yellow ribbon in her hair if she wants to do so. But when the tendency to follow what is considered popular includes the moral and the spiritual, then it becomes very serious. For popularity does not necessarily make for right.

Many boys and girls measure their conduct by popular standards and find themselves stained and soiled by sin and shame.

3. WHAT WILL THE GANG THINK OF IT? is another standard for many. Mary spills her books and Johnny wants to go to her assistance and help her pick them up, but does not dare. The other boys might tease him. The high-school senior does not want to smoke the cigarette someone offers him, but accepts it to please the gang. His standards are created by what the gang wants.

Jesus Christ is the only safe standard by which to live. For almost 2,000 years men and women have tried to find a better yardstick, but always have failed.

Jesus is the way, the life, and the truth. He has set the standards for friendships and love. A love based on the principles of Jesus will endure. It will endure because God is love. All the love in the world comes to us from God.

Jesus set the standards for obedience. He did not want to suffer and die on the cross, but was willing to do so in order to please His heavenly Father. That is why He said, "Nevertheless, not my will, but thine be done."

Jesus is the standard for success. "But he that is greatest among you shall be your servant" (Matthew

23:11). Successful living is always Christian living. No matter how successful you may appear to be you are not successful in the sight of God if you have left Him out. Jesus reminded us of that fact when He asked, "What shall it profit a man if he shall gain the whole world and lose his own soul?"

I want you boys and girls to take Jesus as your yard-stick today and resolve to use Him to measure your life. You may never be able to live up to the highest standards that He has set, but He will lift you up when you fall, and He will walk with you when you are alone. I hope that many of you will do some big things in life, but I know that the biggest thing you can do is to let Jesus come into your heart and live.

24. FIZZ AND FROTH

TEXT: *He that hath ears to hear, let him hear.*
MATTHEW 11:15.

OBJECTS: Two soda-pop bottles: one filled, the other empty.

THE LESSON: We have here two bottles, which remind us of two kinds of boys and girls. One of these bottles is full and ready to fizz over the minute the cap is removed; the other is empty and silent, ready to be filled.

When I see a soda-pop bottle opened, and the froth come fizzing out I think of a certain kind of boys and girls I know. They are soda-pop children who may grow up to be soda-pop men and women.

Perhaps they have done something wrong and their mother says something to them about it, and as soon as she begins to talk to them it is just like taking the top off a soda-pop bottle. They begin to explain how somebody else was to blame and that they themselves are as innocent as babies. They sputter and fizz with all kinds of excuses and explain that it was somebody else who caused them to do the mischief.

I know a boy who sometimes spends so much time watching television or listening to the radio that he fails to study his school lessons properly. But when his mother speaks to him about not getting his lessons, a dozen excuses begin to pop out and he begins to fizz with explanation. The teacher failed to make the assignment clear, or he forgot to bring his history book home from school, or his big sister was playing the piano and he could not concentrate.

If someone tries to tell him the right way to do something he begins to fizz and tell you what he knows about it. He is always so anxious to tell what he knows that you can't get a word in edgewise.

His mother says that he is just like his daddy—wants to talk all the time. Of course, she loves her son dearly and does not mean to be severe with him, but is only trying to tease her husband.

However, unless this boy learns to listen to the advice of those who know more than he does, he will always have a most difficult time managing his own life.

The twelfth chapter of the gospel of Luke tells of a very talkative man who approached Jesus and asked Him to help him with a problem. It seems that his father had died and left some money and his brother had got his fingers on that money and refused to share it with his talkative brother. So when Jesus entered the village the unhappy brother went to Jesus and said, "Speak to my brother and make him divide his inheritance with me."

This man was financially out of luck, and he was miserable and unhappy. His happiness depended on that money. He believed with all his heart that if only he could get his fingers on some of the money he would really be happy, perhaps the happiest man in town. But Jesus knew better. He knew that the man would not be happy even if he had all the inheritance, so He said to him something like this: "God did not make me a judge or a divider over you. Because you are financially out of luck you are miserable and unhappy, but I can tell you about a man who is financially in luck and who is in much worse trouble than you:

"The ground of a certain man brought forth plentifully and he thought within himself saying, What shall I do, because I have no place to store my possessions? And he said, This will I do, I will tear down my old barns and I will build new ones and I will store up much goods for many years and then I will say to my soul, Soul, take thine ease, eat, drink, and be merry. But God said unto him, Thou fool, this day thy soul shall be required of thee, and whose things shall these things be which thou hast provided? So it is with him who layeth up treasures for himself. He is not rich toward God."

Then suddenly Jesus turned awayand left the talkative and unhappy man to draw his own conclusion. So long as the man was doing all the talking and complaining, he was in no position to learn anything.

On one occasion Jesus said, "He that hath ears to hear, let him hear." And on another occasion He said, "Take heed therefore how ye hear." All of you boys and girls, so far as I can see, have ears. Now, since God has given you ears with which to hear He is constantly expecting you to tune in and listen to Him as He speaks to you.

Let us take a last look at these two bottles—one standing ready to overflow at the least provocation. The other is empty and silent—ready to be filled. I hope that you boys and girls will open your minds and your hearts so that Jesus can fill your life with things good and pure.

25. SMALL POTATOES

TEXT: *Let this mind be in you, which was also in Christ Jesus.* PHILIPPIANS 2:5.

OBJECT: A handful of small potatoes.

THE LESSON: We have here a few small potatoes from which we might get a very big lesson. When boys and girls refer to something that is insignificant or inferior they sometimes say, "Oh, that is small potatoes." That is a modern way of saying that the matter in question is of little consequence.

The farm on which I was raised produced many potatoes. When the harvest season arrived my father would run a big turnplow down each row to turn up the potatoes. The potato diggers would follow the plow and gather up the potatoes of marketable size into baskets, and from the baskets fill rows of sacks which stood in line across the fields. The potatoes that had been cut or bruised or were too small to be sold were left on the ground as food for the hogs.

An old man known as Joe living in our neighborhood was always on hand at potato digging time. Joe had never succeeded at anything, but he was always telling other people how to succeed. We youngsters called him Small Potato Joe because he seemed never to see anything but the small potatoes. After we had gathered all the potatoes of marketable value, Small Potato Joe would walk over the fields and complain because we had left so many small potatoes. The hundreds of sacks of good potatoes we had gathered meant nothing to him. All he ever saw were the small potatoes we had left behind.

Although many years have passed since those potato digging days, I can still see Small Potato Joe strutting like a five-star general up and down the rows, pointing with a gnarled finger to the few small potatoes left on the ground. Finding fault with our work seemed to give him a feeling of superiority.

There is no human way to reform a small-potato

mind, because, like the small potatoes, it is always with us. It was a small-potato mind that betrayed Jesus and small-potato diggers who crucified Him on the cross. Even Pilate recognized the treachery of the small-potato mind, but there was little he could do about it.

When Pilate tried to protect Jesus from the fury of the mob they said, "Let his blood be upon us and upon our children." They were perfectly willing to let their children suffer if they could run the show for the moment. Small-potato minds never think about the future or of others. Cain possessed a small-potato mind. He believed that if only he could get his brother Abel out of the way, then he would loom larger in the eyes of God.

We all have in us something of the small-potato complex. There is in each of us an abundance of littleness that drives us to look for the small potatoes in the other fellow's rows. Finding them and pointing them out may well draw attention away from our own failures.

Invariably, the small-potato mind is associated with the most negative forces in every organization. In the work of the church it almost never sees the great missionary program designed to bring light to the dark places of the world. It seldom sees the need for an expansion program to help the next generation have a better and more suitable sanctuary in which to worship God. Rarely does it see Christianity as the greatest force in all the world.

Small Potato Joe has many descendants. Sometimes

a new boy who is nice-looking, a good leader, and a trained singer, comes into a young people's group. The program director gives him a part on the program. He does a splended job. The choir director then asks him to sing a solo, and the congregation responds to his singing. But there is a boy in the group who sees in the new boy a potential threat to his own leadership and egotism. The new boy is getting too much attention. The boy with the small-potato mind begins to look for flaws in the new boy. He does all he can to make the new boy miserable. If only he can get the new boy out of the way his own star will appear a little brighter. The small-potato mind can never see that egotism digs its own grave with the spade of jealousy and envy.

In order that you may be able to identify it I want to give you three major characteristics of the small-potato mind:

1. It looks only for the small potatoes and never sees the big ones that already have been gathered. It never sees the field that is ready for harvesting, because it is too busy searching up and down the rows for the small potatoes someone else has overlooked. If only it can discredit the word of someone else it seems to feel that it has done its service.

2. The small-potato mind invariably looks for the mudhole rather than for the sunrise. It can never find peace and contentment in the presence of bigger minds.

Almost always it allies itself with the great negative forces that are at work, and busies itself with gathering up small potatoes. When we read the Bible and history we soon discover that all of the great forces for good have been positive forces. There are times, of course, when evil gets firmly fixed in the saddle and has to be opposed until it is eliminated, but then it has to be replaced with something positive. Jesus Christ is the world's best example of a great positive mind, and the Bible is still saying to us, "Let the mind of Christ be in you."

26. WHO WANTS A LEMON?

TEXT: *Keep thy heart with all diligence; for out of it are the issues of life.* PROVERBS 4:23.

OBJECT: A lemon.

THE LESSON: It was Monday morning at Cleveland Junior High. A group of boys had gathered around one of their classmates and were watching him with hero-worshiping eyes. They wanted him to tell them about his date with the new girl who had recently moved to town.

"Tell us what she is like," one of the boys pleaded.

"Oh," said the hero of the moment, "she turned out to be a lemon."

While they were talking, the new girl, who looked as neat and tidy as a yellow rose, came walking past the group. They looked sheepishly at each other. She smiled as she hurried by and entered the school building.

To me, she certainly looked more like a tulip or a carnation than a lemon.

There was disappointment in the voice of one boy as he said, "It's a shame that a girl who is so cute to look at has to turn out to be a lemon."

As soon as I reached my study I consulted *Webster's Dictionary*, in which I learned something new about the lemon. The lemon I hold in my hand is classified as a citrus fruit, grown in Florida or California or in some other warm climate. It is noted for its sharp, sour tang. It does not mellow with age nor does it quickly lose its sour taste. Its juice has to be diluted and sweetened before it is pleasant to the taste.

The lemon as a fruit is a very valuable commodity, but when we refer to a person as a lemon we mean, in modern slang, that the person is "a bore; an unpleasant person; an unsatisfying or disappointing person."

It is perfectly possible that the boy was right in saying that the new girl was a lemon, although I have a suspicion that he was merely trying to discourage competition by throwing the other boys off the track.

As I thought of that campus scene I wondered how many of us turn out to be lemons in the sight of God. If, according to Webster's definition, an unpleasant person is a lemon, I wonder how many lemons the Lord finds among us.

A little girl once prayed, "Oh, Lord, please make all of the mean people do good and all of the good people a little more pleasant and a little easier to get along with."

A good many people have the idea that to become a Christian is to become disagreeable and look unhappy. I think we get that idea because perhaps some saints we have known have been so negative in their approach to life and so intolerant of the opinions of others that they have not been as pleasant as Christians should be. They mistakenly think that a good person cannot be a pleasant and lovable person.

One of the great driving forces of the saints of the New Testament was their cheerfulness in the face of danger and hardship. Their religion was a joyous religion. Paul and Silas could sing at midnight from their cell in jail. The face of Stephen was radiant even in his last dying moments. One of the thoughts which Jesus repeatedly tried to drive home was the ideal of cheerfulness. "Be of good cheer, for I have overcome the world."

A lemon may be a disappointing person. I wonder how many of us have been disappointing to God. I think that we are disappointing to God when we listen to the stories about His Son Jesus, and then go on our way refusing to accept Jesus as our Saviour.

I think that we are very disappointing to God when we accept the principles of Jesus but do not adopt them as practical methods by which we are willing to live.

I think that we are very disappointing to God when we permit sins to remain in our hearts without any feeling of shame. And I think we are disappointing to God when we fail to use the talents He has given us. In the parable of the talents Jesus tells of the one-talent man who refused to use his talent, so that it was taken from him and given to the person who had put to profitable use the ten talents that had been given to him. That might sound like an unfair deal, but it is really the way of life.

You boys and girls can avoid the tragedy of being a Christian "lemon" by giving your hearts to Jesus Christ and then living a life of cheerfulness and usefulness in His service.

27. WHERE ARE YOU?

TEXT: *And the Lord God called unto Adam, and said unto him, Where art thou?* GENESIS 3:9.

OBJECT: The following chart printed on a large canvas or cardboard.

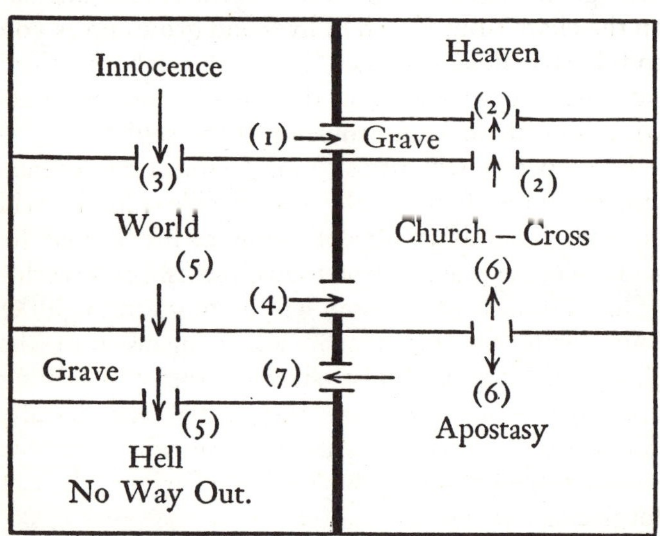

THE LESSON: We have before us this morning a chart which was designed to teach us some of the fundamental doctrines of the Bible concerning the ways by which we may reach our final destination.

The chart is composed of six major compartments, and each compartment represents a state of life—or death. Each person present in this audience is now standing in one of the four of these compartments.

While the Bible teaches that we are all born in sin, it also teaches that we are not held responsible for our sins until we have reached the age of accountability. Therefore, if a child dies in the state of innocence his body passes through gate Number I, from the state of innocence into the grave, and then his soul goes through the second gate into heaven. (Point this out on the chart.) But if a child lives and grows up as you and I have done, he then passes through the third gate and into what we call the world. Here he meets with most of the vital problems of the soul.

Every person who passes from the state of innocence into the state of the world must decide what he will do with Jesus. If he accepts Jesus as his Saviour he will no longer want to live a sinful, selfish, and world-ly life. His next logical step will be to go through the fourth gate and become an active member of the church of his choice. The church is the only existing institution which offers a cross as the way of life. There are many fine institutions in the world, but the church is the only one which offers a Saviour who can forgive us our sins.

You will notice that the cross is located in the same compartment with the church, which is as it should be. It is possible for the cross to exist without the church and as we know it, but it is not possible for the church to exist without real spiritual power and the presence of the cross and all that it symbolizes. The Bible says, "For there is none other name under heaven given among men, whereby we must be saved."

I can imagine that some of you may be secretly asking a question somewhat like this: "Does a person have to belong to a church in order to be saved?"

Now, as much as I believe in the church, I would certainly have to answer such a question in the negative. The organized church as we know it does not have power to save souls. Only God can do that. The church was designed to teach and to preach the word of God and to promote the spirit of Christian fellowship among its members. The church is the mother of all other fine Christian institutions and every Christian should unite with the church and support it. While it is possible for a person to go to heaven and not be a member of the church, it is not possible for a person to go to heaven without the Saviour who died on the cross for the church. In one way or another we all have to reckon with the Christ of the New Testament.

Now, if you have passed from the world into the fellowship of the church you are either a good Christian or a poor one; you either take Jesus seriously or you do not. No one can be half Christian or half sinner. "Ye cannot serve God and mammon." Yet it is possible for a person to be a member of the church and in good and regular standing and still be very pagan in all of his ideals and ideologies.

Some people decide that they will accept Jesus as

their Saviour, so they unite with the church and re-solve to be loyal Christians. For a while they live up to their church membership vows, but then they fall by the wayside, drift down through the fifth gate, and into the state of apostasy—or, if you do not object to the term, we may say that they backslide.

Some say that a person cannot fall from grace, and I believe such is the case; but that does not mean that making a public confession and uniting with the church will forever settle a matter of salvation. While we cannot fall from God's grace, we certainly can refuse it and return to a life of sin. After all of our theological arguments, we all do teach and preach that man is a free moral agent and has the power to choose the road over which he will travel. So long as a person is alive he still has an opportunity to arise from a state of apostasy and return, as did the prodigal son.

Those who have had a religious experience may drift away from God and go through the sixth gate into the state of apostasy. You will notice that this is a two-way street; but if a person dies in this state of apostasy he must then go through the seventh gate into the grave and into eternal damnation, from which there is no escape. But on this side of the grave there is still hope for one who has drifted away from God. He can return to God.

Briefly review the entire chart and list the descriptive Scripture references pertaining to innocence, heaven, hell, the world, the cross, the church, and apostasy. For instance, hell is described as

a prison house
a place of outer darkness
a place which burns with fire and brimstone
a place from which there is no escape
a place where the wealth of the world is of no value
a place from which it is the will of God to save us

The author has used this chart many times before large groups of pioneer campers, youth conferences, and high-school and college audiences, and it has never yet failed to bring forth much interest and many serious questions concerning the ways of salvation.

28. SIGNBOARD RELIGION

TEXT: *Jesus saith unto him, I am the way, the truth, and the life: no man cometh unto the Father but by me.* JOHN 14:6.

OBJECT: A small signboard like those used at highway crossings to designate direction and distance.

THE LESSON: We have here a road sign which is a duplicate of one located on the highway not far from here. The original sign, which says that it is 29 miles to Greenville, also points in the direction of that town. Our highway signs are usually very reliable, but sometimes a thoughtless boy may tamper with a highway sign and cause a motorist endless confusion.

After the famous battle of Dunkirk many of the English people felt that it would be only a matter of time before the Germans would succeed in landing on English soil. In order to hamper their movement in such an event, English boys and girls went to work to reverse the road signs on the highways. Fortunately, the Germans did not make the attempt.

Something like that seems to have happened to many of us today. Many of the moral and spiritual signboards on which we have learned to depend now seem to be wholly unreliable. Only a generation ago boys and girls were taught to believe that whiskey is a definitely harmful habit-forming stimulant. Now many of the advertisements in our favorite magazines tell us that drinking is the privilege of people of distinction.

Preachers used to tell us that sin was a condition of the heart and that we had to repent of our sins before we could find any peace within ourselves or even with God. But today we are told by many so-called leading authorities that our miseries and warped minds are caused by something which happened far back in our childhood, that we are just innocent victims of our environment and are not really to blame for our conduct.

It is all so confusing that we may sometimes wish that we had some definite signboards on which to rely.

Well, we do have! Jesus' teaching is the standard by which we must live if we hope to reach the goal of happiness and eternal salvation.

When Jesus told His disciples that He was going away, they were all confused. They thought that He had come to set up an earthly kingdom, and now He was about to leave them. Then "Thomas saith unto him, Lord, we know not whither thou goest; and how can we know the way?"

And Jesus replied, "I am the way, the truth, and the life: no man cometh unto the Father, but by me."

Jesus is still the way to happiness. You may lie and cheat and steal if you will, but you cannot do these things and still be happy. Sin and happiness cannot live in the same soul together. Sin is so selfish that it can never rest until happiness has been kicked out.

Jesus is the truth about God. Some time, when we read in the Old Testament about how the bears came out of the woods and ate up forty-two little boys because they mocked Elisha and called him "Old Bald Head," we may shudder and wonder what God really is like. But then, when we study the life of Jesus, we see what God is like. God is like Jesus. Jesus said that. "He that hath seen me hath seen the Father."

Then He says, "I am the way. I am the road. You will walk along with me all the way from where you are today to the home of the soul. Start from where you are and follow the road to where it leads. If you are baffled by the conflicting signs just keep going, for I am the way.

"I am the way—the road to travel on; I am the truth —the reliable map and guidebook, the road sign and the markers. Let people tamper with the moral and spiritual road signs if they will, but you keep plugging on."

He shows us the way. He tells us how to walk in it. He makes it possible for us to continue on our journey.

He will not mock us with a vision which cannot be realized. Lost boys and girls can be saved. The unclean can be made clean. The weak can be made strong. If you will follow the well-marked road of salvation Jesus will walk with you—all the way.

29 LET FREEDOM RING

TEXT: *And the chief captain answered, With a great sum obtained I this freedom. And Paul said, But I was free born.* ACTS 22:28.

OBJECTS: A Bible and a piece of chain.

THE LESSON: These two objects—a Bible and a chain—do not seem to have any direct connection with each other, and yet they have existed side by side throughout the ages. The chain is the symbol of the power of Satan and slavery and the Bible is the symbol of Christ and freedom.

It is difficult for us in America to understand and appreciate the meaning of freedom. We have been used to freedom so long that it is difficult for us to imagine what it might be like to have to live as serfs of some power. But this freedom that we enjoy and often take for granted has not always existed.

In the early days of Christianity there were many millions of slaves in the Roman Empire. Often, when a Roman general defeated a country, he would take all the fine and promising boys and girls, as well as the more talented adults, to Rome to serve as slaves. Even those who were permitted to remain in their native countries were not allowed to live with their parents. Many of them were farmed out to the Roman officials who came to govern the conquered people.

Some of the slaves fared very well; others fared less well. But all of them were chained in a very real sense; they could not come and go except as their masters gave them permission. Chances for a slave to regain his freedom were very remote.

Many of the slaves began to search for something that would enable them the better to endure their chains, and they found it in the Word of God. God took the bitterness and the resentment out of their hearts and gave them peace and joy, which baffled their masters.

As the principles of the New Testament found their way into the hearts of more people, the Word of God became more powerful than the chains of slavery. Gradually the chains of slavery have given way to the Word of God, until human slavery cannot legally exist where the influence of Christ has gone.

As we look at these two objects—the Bible and the chain—we realize that they symbolize the two great powers which are seeking to control the lives of everybody. Satan is trying to bind us with chains and fetters, and Jesus is trying to help us escape from those bonds.

The chain of ignorance is very strong. Millions of people in the world do not know about Jesus. Many of them live in constant fear lest the evil powers do harm. Our missionaries know that the Word of God is the only power strong enough to break the chain of ignorance. As the Word of God begins to live in the hearts of the ignorant their chains begin to weaken. Their fears give way to faith. The more they learn about the Bible, the less they fear the powers of evil.

But you boys and girls do not have to go to Africa or to India to see an example of how sin binds people until they cannot free themselves. All about us we can see people who have become victims of bad habits from which they would like to be free. They may pull and tug at the old chains, but the chains usually hold fast. But we need not despair if we are really willing to give the Word of God a chance to operate in our lives.

Sin is a chain that binds its victim. The Word of God is like a liberator who comes to take off the chains.

A few years ago, while she was on her way home from school, a couple of hoodlums kidnapped a high-school senior. They took her to an old abandoned mill, where they chained her to a post before going out to try to collect a ransom from her father. In the meantime FBI agents were diligently searching for the missing girl. When the hoodlums returned to the mill, they found that their captive had been set free by the agents of the FBI, who immediately arrested them and put them behind bars.

God is more diligent than the smartest agents of the Federal Bureau of Investigation. His eyes are always running to and fro over the earth, seeking to make Himself strong in us. Any time we want to be free of our sins, God will free us of them. God is truth. And let us remember that Jesus said, "Know the truth, and the truth will make you free."

30. KNOW YOUR ONIONS

TEXT: *And ye shall know the truth, and the truth shall make you free.* JOHN 8:32

OBJECTS: Several onions of different varieties and sizes placed in a glass jar for display.

THE LESSON: The student was paying his English teacher a very high compliment when he said, "She knows her onions." To know your onions means, according to *Webster's Dictionary*, "to have a strong knowledge of some subject; to be highly skilled along some particular line; to be clever at one's business or profession; to possess all-around intelligence; to be efficient."

Here we have a jar of onions of different sizes and varieties. As most folks know, the onion is a source of a most effective tear gas, which affects the eyes. The eyes then send a message to the tear glands, "Onion gas—send tears, please." When the tears flow over the eyeball, they form a film which shut out the irritating onion gas from direct contact with the nerves of the eye, and so prevent injury to them. Such information concerning the onion might be interesting, but is hardly necessary. You may or may not literally know these onions, but you should know your onions when the fundamental principles of life are concerned.

It is necessary for you to know your onions concerning the Bible. The Bible is God's Holy Word, and it is the basic means by which we come to know God. We know that the Bible came from God, because if we follow its teachings it will lead us back to God. When we study the Bible, we discover how God revealed Himself to us.

The Bible not only tells us about the creation and the fall of mankind, it also tells of man's redemption through the saving power of Jesus Christ. The Bible has an answer for every problem and a Saviour for every sin.

The Bible is the word of God expressed in the lives of men who suffered from every sort of human temptation. According to the story of Joseph Smith, the Mormon Bible was found already written, carefully preserved in a sacred box. The leaves of the Bible were plates of pure gold, bound together by three golden rings, and on top of the book was a rather remarkable equipment—a pair of supernatural spectacles through which Joseph Smith alone could look and read. While looking through these supernatural spectacles, he read the Word of God, copied it and gave the world the Mormon Bible. Or, at least, that is one of the stories we hear about it.

There is also an interesting story concerning how the Mohammedans got their Bible. The angel Gabriel is said to have brought Mohammed the Bible page by page and to have remained by his side while he copied the pages. Then the angel took the pages of the Bible back to heaven, where they are still under lock and key. That is the story of how the Mohammedans got their Bible.

We did not get our Bible like that. Every page of our Bible was written by human fingers. It came to us out of the furnace of human hearts. It is alive with the vital struggles of men and women who met temptations, faced duty, bore burdens, faced sorrows. It throbs with the anguish, the penitence, the pain, and loneliness, the tragedy, the high thoughts, the wretched failures, and the spiritual triumphs of men.

Here is a man who has muffed the ball. He has made a miserable failure of life, and we hear him crying out, "Oh that I had wings like a dove! for then would I fly away, and be at rest." Seemingly he is beaten to earth. Then down on his knees he goes, and now he is saying, "I waited patiently for the Lord; and he inclined unto me, and heard my cry. He brought me up also out of a horrible pit, out of the miry clay, and set my feet upon a rock, and established my goings. And he hath put a new song in my mouth, even praise unto our God." The man writes out that experience, and it has become a part of our Bible. So I say to you boys and girls you should know your onions concerning the Bible and what it teaches about God and man.

You should also know your onions concerning the art of worship. Some people think that worship consists of attending the services of the church, bowing their heads in prayer, joining in singing the hymns, and sitting while the minister preaches. All these things are quite necessary to the spirit of worship, but a person may do all these things and still never know the meaning of worship. True worship is an honest effort to tune in on God's wave length so that we may hear the message He has for us. Sitting in church and listening to a sermon is not necessarily worshiping God. The true worshiper seeks to find God's will for him.

Then, too, you should know your onions concerning how to get the most out of prayer. I recently heard a bicycle rider in a circus say that he had learned to ride a bicycle by taking a correspondence course. Well, you might learn to become a good bicycle rider by taking a correspondence course, but you cannot learn the art of praying by reading a book about prayer. For true prayer is an attitude of mind seeking to learn the will of God, or an humble desire to serve God in some capacity or to secure His merciful favor for loved ones. Here is a good sermon on prayer.

Prayer is asking.
Prayer is asking God.
Prayer is asking God for something definite.
Prayer is asking God for something definite which is in keeping with His will.

What you actually know about the onion is insignificant, but that you understand the meaning of the slang expression is vitally important. It is vitally important that you know your onions concerning the Bible, the art of worship, and the attitude of prayer.

31. THE COLOR OF YOUR COAT

TEXT: *Now Israel loved Joseph more than all his children, because he was the son of his old age: and he made him a coat of many colours.* GENESIS 37:3.

OBJECT: A chart containing the various colors which Joseph's coat might have contained.

THE LESSON: We have here a very colorful chart, but we do not claim that it is as colorful as the coat which Jacob made for his son Joseph. That coat caused young Joseph no end of trouble. Every boy and girl knows the story of Joseph, favorite son of his father, and the object of so much jealousy among his brothers that they sold him to a band of Ishmaelites, who took him as a slave to far-away Egypt. How Joseph managed to rise from the position of a slave to one of power and prominence in Egypt is one of the most thrilling stories in the Bible. Right now we want to think about the coat of many colors which Jacob made for Joseph and see how it reminds us of some of the colors we made for ourselves.

Every boy and girl has a coat of many colors which no one but God ever sees. You make your coat of the things you think and do. Your every experience becomes part of its material.

The coat which you make for yourself may have some green in it, because green stands for jealousy. Jealousy is one of the oldest and most vicious sins in all the world. We see it playing a part in the lives of Adam and Eve. When the cunning serpent told Eve that to eat of the forbidden fruit would make her wise, she disobeyed God and partook of the fruit. She felt that God's restrictions were robbing her of much pleasure. The devil is constantly attempting to convince us that he who lives in sin has more fun than the Christian, which is not true.

Just outside of the Garden of Eden we see Abel prospering, while his brother Cain is not so prosperous. When Cain put on the green coat of jealousy, he decided to kill his brother Abel. His idea seemed to be to get Abel out of the way so that he might win favor with God. But, instead of winning favor with God, he brought severe punishment down on his own head. His coat of jealousy at last brought him only shame and disgrace. We may be sure that the coat which Joseph made for himself had no green in it. When we begin to wear the green coat of jealousy we are heading for trouble.

Some coats have large patches of red, which symbolizes a quick temper. Now, before you boast of your temper, you should know that an uncontrollable temper is not a characteristic of which we should boast. The greatest display of uncontrollable temper is often seen in an insane asylum. The more intelligent a person is, the better is he able to control his temper. Temper is a fine virtue to possess, but we must possess it and not let it possess us. When we let our tempers possess us, then they become great handicaps.

Some coats have large streaks of yellow in them. Yellow is a symbol of cowardice, a trait which is despised by both saint and sinner. As we read the story of the life of Joseph we know that there were no yellow streaks in the coat he made for himself, for he was a man of great moral courage.

Some coats are spotted with black patches, which tell of lies and trickery. But we may be sure that Joseph did not stain his coat with the blackness of trickery and untruthfulness.

When Joseph was taken to Egypt he was forced to leave his coat of many colors behind. But Joseph made another coat of many colors of the things he thought, said, and did, and that was the coat which God saw and admired.

Joseph put in his coat of many colors some white for purity, which comes from clean thinking. If any man ever had a right to think mean and ugly thoughts that man was Joseph. He had been treated unfairly by his own brothers, and he might easily have filled his heart with thoughts of revenge, but he did not. Instead of becoming sour and belligerent, he put his trust in God and filled his mind with clean thoughts.

I am sure that Joseph put in his coat of many colors some purple, which symbolizes the nobility which comes from forgiveness and fairness. Years after his brothers had robbed him of the coat which his father

Jacob had made for him, and had sold him to the Ishmaelite traders, those same brothers were forced to go to far-away Egypt in search of food. There Joseph, who was by that time one of the most powerful men in all Egypt, recognized them and was willing to forgive them and to help them. There was no bitterness in his soul and no desire to get even with them for what they had done to him.

So you see each of you has a coat of many colors. What are the colors of your coat? What colors does God see when He looks at you? The Bible says, "Man looketh upon the outward appearance, but God looketh upon the heart." Are you making a bright coat, or is it stained with jealousy, deceit, anger, pride? Look again at the colors of your coat.

32. EASTER DAWNS

TEXT: *He that hath seen me hath seen the father.*
JOHN 14:9.

OBJECTS: A basket of easter eggs.

THE LESSON: Easter is here again and how happy everyone is. Some are happy because they have new dresses, others because school is out, and still others because they are alive on this glad springtime morning, when the heavens and the earth declare the glory of God in leaves and flowers.

But the greatest event of all to be happy about is

that for which Easter eggs stand. They stand for the greatest event in history—the resurrection of Jesus Christ, our Lord and Saviour. When we put eggs under a hen or in an incubator to hatch they look so cold and silent that it seems as if they might be little tombs in which only death abides.

But inside each egg is a little germ of life. By the warmth that surrounds the egg night and day for about twenty-one days that germ of life grows and begins to stir. Finally, a fluffy little chicken will peck his way out of his little shell, and what resembled a tiny tomb turns out to be a cradle of life.

Something like that happened to Jesus. God wanted His people to know Him and understand Him. God revealed Himself to His people in dreams and visions, but the people failed to understand what He was like. He then tried to reveal Himself through prophets, but the wicked people refused to listen to the prophets. He tried to reveal Himself through a series of judges, but the people did not respond to the teaching of the judges. Then He tried to reveal Himself through kings, but still the people did not understand what God was like.

So at last He decided to send His own beloved Son to earth so that the people might really know what God was like. But when Jesus came and said, "He that hath seen me hath seen the Father," even then the people did not understand that God was like Jesus. A few people believed on Him and accepted Him as their Saviour, but most of them rejected Him.

His enemies decided that it was time to get rid of

Him, so they crucified Him on the cross, and then His friends placed His body in a tomb. It was a sad day for those who loved Jesus, for they believed that He was really dead.

For three days the tomb was cold and silent. But on the third day, which was Easter morning, when Mary went to the tomb she found that it was empty. An angel had come and rolled the stone away from the entrance of the tomb, and Jesus had walked out triumphant over death. Mary was standing near the tomb weeping, and when someone asked her why she was weeping she said that somebody had taken the body of her Lord away and she did not know where they had hidden it. But Mary was wrong. Nobody had stolen the body of Jesus. An angel had come and rolled the stone away, and Jesus had walked out triumphant over death and was there in her presence. But her eyes were so filled with tears that she was not then able to see Him.

After Jesus revealed Himself to His disciples they began to understand the meaning of the salvation that Jesus had proclaimed to them. He had told them that if they would believe on Him and accept Him as their Saviour He would come into their hearts and would be like a germ of eternal life.

When Jesus Himself arose from the grave it was as though He said to them, "This is what I mean. I have in my soul the germ of eternal life. And since that is true, death as you know it cannot touch me. They may put my body in a tomb and seal the tomb, but nobody can seal up my soul. That is what I have been trying to show you. Now accept me as your Saviour, and then your soul will be in the hands of God."

You may be sure that all the friends of Jesus were very happy on that first Easter morning. And every Easter since that glorious day has been a happy time for the friends of Jesus because of His victory over death.

Easter reminds us that we too can have eternal life. Jesus had to suffer and die in order to make us understand what God is really like. Now when we are confused about the nature of God we can look on Jesus and remember that He said, "He that hath seen me hath seen the Father."

33. GOOD OR BAD?

TEXT: *The lip of truth shall be established for ever.* PROVERBS 12:19.

OBJECTS: A large butcher knife, a silver dollar, and a small Bible.

THE LESSON: I hold in my hand a large butcher knife and I want you to help me decide whether it is a good thing or a bad thing. Let us suppose that your mother has just baked a large turkey but has no knife with which to carve it and you are extremely hungry. Then someone comes in and places this knife in your hand. Would it be a good thing or a bad thing? Of course you will all agree that it would be a very good thing under such circumstances. But suppose that we should go out and find a man who was insane or angry enough to kill someone and we should place the knife in his hand. Would it then be a good thing or a bad thing?

Or let us consider this silver dollar. (Display the dollar.) Suppose I should become generous and big-hearted and place this dollar in your hands and should say to you "It is yours." Would the dollar be a good thing or a bad thing? Of course you would think it would be a good thing. But suppose I should go out and buy a dollar's worth of carpet tacks and scatter them up and down the street so that they might be picked up by an automobile tire. Would the dollar still be a good thing or a bad thing? Or suppose that I should bury this dollar and forget where I put it. Would it then be good or bad?

I am sure that you can see that the knife is useful that it is neither good nor bad but can be used for any purpose you desire. The same is true of the dollar. It is useful—neither good nor bad but can be used for a good purpose or a bad purpose.

When you have a dollar to spend you are going to exchange it for what you want most. Yesterday I saw a man whose shoes were worn out. Yet he went into a liquor store and came out with a bottle of whiskey. He needed shoes and no doubt wanted them, but there was another desire which was greater. A man might want a new radio when his taxes become due, but he would rather pay his taxes than to suffer the penalty for refusing to pay them. When, then, he chooses freedom from debt rather than a new radio, that is what he wants most.

If you boys and girls want to please Jesus, you will remember that it is your duty to give a part of your weekly allowance to help promote the work of the Lord. This coin is neither good nor bad, but we can use it to promote goodness or we can use it to promote evil.

Now, the same thing is true of this Bible. It is the Word of God and it gives us the progressive revelation of God from the creation of the world to His atonement for our sins on the cross. It also tells us something about the troubles of the early church and of how its leaders suffered and died for the causes for which the church was established. Its real value to you will depend on how you use it. If you will read it, believe it, apply its teaching to your own lives, and will let God speak to you through its pages, it will then become like a lamp unto your feet and a light unto your pathway. But if you simply let it lie on a table unopened to catch dust, it will mean very little to you. The Bible is not to be used as a charm but as food for the soul.

The best food in the world is of little value until we eat it and digest it, and it becomes absorbed in our blood stream to make needed energy. The Word of God is spiritual food. We must digest it, and absorb it in our blood stream before we can produce fruit for the Master. David was getting at the core of the matter when he said, "Thy word have I hid in mine heart, that I might not sin against thee." May we learn to say and do the same.

34. GRAPEVINE STORIES

TEXT: *But the tongue can no man tame.* JAMES 3:8.

OBJECTS: A piece of grapevine. Or any vine will do.

THE LESSON: Quite often we hear a bit of surprising news and learn from our informant that it came "over the grapevine."

Of course, we all know that we cannot literally hear anything over a grapevine, or, for that matter, over any vine. If I were to ask one of you boys and girls to listen to the stories which this piece of vine (demonstrate) might tell you I am sure that the idea would seem absurd to you. And yet you probably listen frequently to stories which are reported to have come to you "over the grapevine."

The grapevine as a system of communication has come to mean the channel over which confidential gossip or idle rumors may travel. Since we all live in a world in which the grapevine system of communication is in almost constant use, I think we might well consider some of the facts about grapevine stories.

1. A grapevine story is usually an ugly story—one which is definitely harmful to someone. Stories which

are designed to help people do not usually travel over the grapevine system. If someone should tell me that one of you boys or girls had won a scholarship I would congratulate you, be proud of you, and would probably go out and share the good news with my friends. Stories that are helpful, that bring pride or glory to people, can always stand the test of publicity. That is true because there is nothing in them we want to conceal. But a harmful story usually cannot stand the test of publicity and so it travels over the grapevine system of communication. No one can hold anybody responsible for a grapevine story, because there is almost no way to trace its origin. Shortly after I was called to my first pastorate a grapevine story was started which said that I had publicly denounced the mayor of our town for his conduct in office. The mayor happened to be an officer in the church I was serving. The news was buzzing all over town that the new preacher had publicly rebuked the man for attending church while under the influence of liquor. There was not one word of truth in the story.

"I mean to get to the bottom of this story," I said to the mayor, " and find out who started it."

"Son," the mayor replied, "Just remember that you can't go to the bottom of a garbage can in search of rottenness without getting your hands soiled on the way down. You can't trace a grapevine story, and even if you could, it wouldn't cause anybody to reform. Pay no attention to the story and go on with your work. I know the story is not true. You know it is not true. My friends know that it is not true, and my political enemies would not believe the truth if they heard it, so the best thing for you to do, young man, is to forget the story and get on with your work." That was good advice.

2. Grapevine stories are almost always erroneous. They cannot stand the test of truth. They may deal with a good many facts in the beginning, but the more they are repeated, the more the facts are likely to become warped and twisted. A beloved minister of my acquaintance was a victim of such a story. One night youthful pranksters gathered up some empty whiskey bottles and deposited them on his lawn. The next morning his wife gathered them up and threw them into the garbage can. She didn't even mention the incident to her husband. When the garbage collector saw the empty bottles in the minister's garbage can he took them out and gave them to one of the deacons in the church the minister was serving. Yes, the minister had certainly taken to drinking whiskey; here was the proof: the empty whiskey bottles had been found in his garbage can. That was the conclusion of the garbage collector. Fortunately, the deacon did not believe the story, but no doubt a good many other people did. It was true that empty whiskey bottles were found in the minister's garbage can, but the whole truth threw a different light on the matter.

3. Grapevine stories should not be repeated. Many people who will gladly repeat an ugly grapevine story would not think of originating such a story. The fact that it has been told to us need not make us feel that it is all right to pass it on to a friend. Someone has sug-

gested that the following test for *every* story or bit of gossip might well be used before we repeat it:

1. Is it helpful? If you repeat a grapevine story will it help anyone? If the story is of such a nature that it will not help anyone, then it certainly should not be passed on.

2. Is it harmful? Few grapevine stories we hear are neutral. Any story which is not helpful is almost certain to be harmful. Even if we know that a grapevine story is true we should not repeat it if its repetition will not bring peace and joy to others. The very fact that it is repeated in whispers would suggest that it might be harmful to someone. Stories which do not involve character and reputation of others seldom travel over the grapevine system.

3. Is it true? Before we repeat a story concerning the character or conduct of another person we should be certain that it is true. If there is doubt that it is true we should not repeat it. Finally, is it always necessary to let grapevine gossip pass your lips? The advice that the Apostle Paul gave a long time ago is still good: "Whatsoever things are true, whatsoever things are honest, whatsoever things are just, whatsoever things are pure, whatsoever things are lovely, whatsoever things are of good report; if there be any virtue, and if there be any praise, think on these things."

35. TO GIVE THE OLD BRUSH-OFF

TEXT: *Take fast hold of instruction; let her not go: keep her; for she is thy life.* PROVERBS 4: 13.

OBJECT: A clothes brush.

THE LESSON: A high-school student was telling his girl friend how he had managed to give his parents the brush-off when they wanted him to stay in and study his lessons. His fluffy little girl friend gave him a very bright smile, indicating that she thought he had done a very wonderful thing.

We have here a clothes brush—a very useful household article. If I should hand this brush to one of you and ask you to give it to your parents you would perhaps gladly comply with my request. But if I had not made such a request and then should hear one of you say that you had given your parents the brush-off I would not think of a little brush such as I am now holding in my hand.

To give one "the brush-off" means, in modern slang, to disregard or reject, as advice, suggestion, or even one's company. One of the strongest urges inside every boy and girl is to disregard or reject parents' advice. You young people differ in many ways, but one thing is true of each of you—you want to be independent, to be your own boss, and not be pushed around by older people.

Some of you may be having trouble with your parents. Recently I ran across a piece of paper on which my young daughter had written out some New Year's resolutions. One of them was to be more patient with her parents during the coming year. You want to do things which your parents think you should not do. You make plans, but they keep interfering with your plans and saying, "You must not do this and you must not do that." And you want to make your own decisions; you want to be free, not to be hemmed in by parental rules and regulations. So you are strongly tempted at times to reject your parents' advice, brush it off, and go on doing as you please.

When you are faced with such temptations just remember that your parents are just as anxious as you are for you to grow up and be free and independent. Their hearts would be broken if they thought that you could never get away from your mother's apron strings. But they know that life can be cruel, and they want you to learn to handle your freedom gradually, so that you may avoid some of the pitfalls of life.

You boys and girls are just like boys and girls of the past in that sometimes you may feel that your parents are very old and antiquated in their thinking. When your parents tell you what they used to do when they were young people, you may listen with a great degree of interest but with little desire to attempt to duplicate their experiences. Some time you may say to yourself, "Well, that's not the way we do things today."

Many modern boys and girls feel that their parents are so far behind the times that even though they may be very sincere their advice just isn't suitable for to-day.

Once I stood in the shipyard at Norfolk, Virginia, and watched a new ship as it sailed out to sea. With its shining paint, and armored sides and flying flags, it was beautiful to behold as it glided through the water.

The years will pass and some day that ship will be old. And when the new ship becomes an old ship it will be scarred and battered by the pounding seas and the lashing gales.

Like an old ship, your parents have been through the stormy seas of life. They know that you too will soon run into some rough seas, and they know how cruel the storms can be.

Before you reject the advice of your parents you might well remember that they love you better than does anyone else on earth, and they sincerely want to help you find the greatest happiness in life. Most of them would gladly make any sacrifice, even life itself, if by so doing they might save you from a life of misery.

Another thing to remember when you are tempted to give your parents the brush-off is this: There is no such thing as total freedom in this world. When you are free from the controls of your parents you will still not be free to do as you please. Your school-teacher, your employer, the income tax man, even the policeman on the corner may have something to say about what you do or do not do.

Freedom is not escaping from controls, for every decent life has to be controlled. *Pinocchio* runs away from home and escapes all sorts of external restraints, but he does not get away from *Jimminy Cricket*, his conscience. *Jimminy Cricket* goes along, and if *Pinocchio* does not let *Jimminy Cricket* control him from the inside, then he had far better be back where someone controlled him from the outside. Every time *Pinocchio* gets too far away from his conscience he finds himself in all kinds of trouble.

Charley McCarthy said that he was sick and tired of being merely an echo of Edgar Bergen's voice. His New Year's resolution was to get out from under Bergen's control so that he could be free. But I am sure that *Charley* could not get very far without Bergen's control.

If we cannot be controlled from the inside, then we will have to be controlled from the outside. Your parents may seem old-fashioned and out of date in many ways, but they will never knowingly give you advice that will rob you of your happiness. And just as soon as you show signs of being able to control your own conduct they will be happy to grant you your freedom.

36. THE WAY OF THE CHISELER IS HARD

TEXT: *The way of transgressors is hard.* PROVERBS 13:15.

OBJECTS: A small wooden mallet and a chisel.

THE LESSON: We have here a chisel and a mallet. If I were to place the chisel against the corner of the pew, pulpit, or the organ and begin to pound away on it with this mallet, much damage would result. But no matter how much damage I might inflict with this chisel and mallet, I would not be called a chiseler. A chiseler is something else.

The word "chiseler" is a slang term used to describe a person who refuses to follow the rules of good conduct. Webster says that to chisel is "to cheat; to evade compliance with the law; to use dishonest or unjust methods to gain one's end; to pay undue attention to a member of the opposite sex who is already engaged or married."

The way of the chiseler is always hard. Adam and Eve decided that they could afford the risk of disobeying eternal laws. Instead of doing exactly what God told them to do, Eve yielded to the voice of the serpent, which assured her that if she would eat the forbidden fruit she would become wise like the gods. But after Adam and Eve had eaten the forbidden fruit they were ashamed, so they hid themselves. After they had sinned they could no longer feel comfortable in the presence of God.

Sin always separates man from God. When one begins to chisel away at God's eternal laws he often begins to feel so uncomfortable in church that he is apt to start looking for an excuse to quit attending. I am convinced that almost all the petty reasons people give for not attending church are merely excuses intended to justify their failure.

In the New Testament we read the story of two chiselers, Ananias and his wife Sapphira, who agreed to sell their house and land and turn the proceeds over to the general fund the apostles had set up. But after they sold their property, the money looked so good to them that they changed their minds and decided to keep a part of it. When they arrived at the appointed place bringing only a part of the proceeds from the sale of their property, Peter reminded them that they had lied to God. Then both fell dead at the feet of the apostles. The way of the chiseler is usually very hard.

Some of us attempt to chisel on the Lord when it comes to our church membership vows. We accept the Lord as our Saviour and promise that we will be His faithful followers; then we attempt to avoid keeping our promises. We promise to support the church and its work, but go no further than lip service. Or perhaps we decide to take God into our lives as an economic partner and give Him a tithe of our increase as did Jacob of old. We follow the practice for a little while and then dissolve our partnership with the Lord. Then one day we get into a tight place and would give anything if only we had a partner whose resources were unlimited. But we have dissolved the relationship with the Lord, and must face our problems alone. The way of the chiseler is hard.

Then some attempt to chisel on the moral laws. They pretend to be good and religious and loyal to the standards of Jesus, but their thoughts and deeds are evil. Their lips, the lips through which they pray, are given to profanity and lies. The eyes which should behold the good see only the evil, the cheap, the tarnished. The ears which should listen to the Word of God hear the voice of Satan. The feet which walk down the church aisle on Sunday morning walk into a saloon on Monday. The hand that gives in lovely benevolence also wounds in jealousy or malice. The voice that praises may also be the voice that curses.

We need to remember the words of the Master, who said that a good tree cannot produce evil fruit. He also said that a good spring cannot produce bitter water. We may chisel on God's Kingdom, but God's Kingdom will stand.

A man watched a blacksmith pounding away on an anvil. He wondered how long it would take the blacksmith to wear away the anvil. The blacksmith said that the anvil wore out the hammers, but itself withstood the blows. So it is with God's Word. For ages skeptics have beaten on God's anvil, but the anvil stands, while the skeptics come and go.

A few years ago there were signs along the highways which said, "Don't be a chiseler." That advice might well apply to every one of us when we deal with the eternal laws of God.

37. THE GATES OF HEAVEN*

TEXT: *On the east three gates; on the north three gates; on the south three gates; and on the west three gates.* REVELATION 21:13.

OBJECT: A large cardboard box with three doors or gates cut in each side. Let each side represent one of the directions mentioned in the Scripture text.

THE LESSON: The author of the Book of Revelation gives us a vivid picture of the various gates through which we may enter the home of the soul. It matters not which gate you use, because all lead to the foot of the cross on which Jesus died. "For there is none other name under heaven given among men whereby we may be saved" (Acts 4:12).

"On the east three gates; on the north three gates; on the south three gates; and on the west three gates." This is the inspired poet's description of the Way of Salvation. He is thinking in terms of a home for the

* This object lesson is based on a radio address delivered some years ago by the late Dr. Hugh T. Kerr.

soul to which the redeemed of God may come. It is a vision, a revelation, a picture of redemption.

An interesting thing about the picture is that the gates of heaven are flung wide open to all the world. There are twelve gates to the eternal city, three on the east, three on the north, three on the south, and three on the west, none of which is ever closed. The gates are open to all who would enter the Kingdom of God.

While Jesus emphasized that there are only two final destinations and one major road leading to each, this prophet tells us there are many little paths leading into roads that run into these two major highways. The little path of social drinking may lead us into the highway of alcoholism; the little path of selfishness may lead us into the highway of greed; the little path of intolerance may lead us into the highway of Pharisaism; the little path of careless habits may lead us into the highway of sin over which multitudes of people are traveling.

So the little paths of prayer and devotion and repentance and forgiveness may lead us to the narrow way and strait gate—on to the feet of Jesus. Let us now take a look at these various gates.

Each of us must travel the path which appeals to him most and must come over his own road to the feet of Jesus. His experience is his own and is unlike the experience of any other man. The Apostle Paul and St. Augustine, Dwight L. Moody and John Wesley, Phillips Brooks and Horace Bushnell, Stanley Jones and Billy Graham, each finds Christ in his own way and hears Christ speak in his own tongue.

This is a thought we need to remember. It is all too easy for us to demand that everyone shall have the same experience, walk over the same path, and enter at the same gate. While we all must find the same refuge in the same Saviour, we do not have to travel over the same path to get to the feet of Jesus.

Jesus Himself made this thought crystal clear in His parables. He tells of a man who found a treasure hidden in a field. The man was not searching for the treasure. It was the great surprise of his life when his plowshare hit it. But it was his discovery and he was willing to sacrifice all that he possessed in order to keep it.

Again, the Kingdom of God is like the pearl of great price, in the story of the merchant who was seeking goodly pearls, and having found one of tremendous value went and sold all that he had and bought it. This man had found the pearl of great price, not by accident, but because he was searching diligently for it.

There are real parables of life. Here is a man whose soul is troubled and he begins to search for peace of mind. He tried many things, and finally comes face to face with Jesus, and then knows that he has found the real thing. So he gives up his old life and begins to be a disciple of Jesus. But here is another man, who goes to a revival meeting because he is curious and while he is there God touches his heart and he finds the way of Jesus. The danger is that we are always trying to force our own experience on someone else, while Jesus takes us where we are, and as we are, and leads us into His presence.

I. THE WEST GATE

Some enter the Kingdom through the gate which faces the west. Now, the west has ever represented storms and thunder and clouds and mystery.

When a Puritan died his friends would say that he had "gone west," and often the dead were buried facing the east, the point of sunrise.

It was through the West Gate that Paul entered the Kingdom of God. His was a startling experience. A dazzling light blinded him and he heard the voice of God speaking to him. And then he felt the weight of the cross fall from him and he knew that God had saved his soul. The West Gate is the way of the great revivals which have swept through our church under the leadership of saintly men like Sam Jones, Billy Sunday, Cyclone Mack, and many other great evangelists. Many of you have come to God through some great experience in a revival. And we thank God for this West Gate through which the burdened sinner can come and find pardon at the feet of Jesus.

II. THE NORTH GATE

Some enter the Kindgom through the North Gate. The north represents the cold and calculating dispositions which demand a *reasonable faith*. They must know and understand. Things must be made clear to them. They stand in the company of Nicodemus, who asked, "How can these things be?" They stand with

Thomas, who said, "Except I shall see in his hands the print of the nails . . . I will not believe."

Now we see that Jesus did not argue with Nicodemus, but simply said to him, "Ye must be born again." We do not hear directly again from Nicodemus until we see him standing with the redeemed around the crucified body of Jesus. And I cannot believe that Jesus thought any less of Thomas because Thomas demanded proof of His real existence, for Jesus did show great patience when He gave Thomas the evidence for which the doubting apostle was looking.

The Ethiopian was searching diligently for the Master when the evangelist Philip patiently read to him from the Book and explained to him something of the greatness of God. I have great sympathy for those who enter the Kingdom of God through the North Gate, for it is a gate which represents honest thinking and an honest endeavor to find the truth, and Jesus is still saying to all burdened souls, "Come unto me, all ye that labor and are heavy laden, and I will give you rest."

III. THE SOUTH GATE

Others enter the Kingdom through the gate that faces the south. The south is the place of the winsome ways of spring and summer sunshine. The south is the land of flowers and blossoms and all of the loveliness of nature. When bleak winter comes, the wild geese fly south because they want to find warmth and sunshine. A multitude whom no man can number has come to Christ out of this summer land and entered through the South Gate.

It was through the South Gate that I came to Christ. It was through the South Gate that, perhaps, a number of you have come to Christ. And we can stand proudly in the group with Timothy, who knew the Scriptures from childhood and had been led into the Kingdom by the prayers, and through the influence of Christian parents. Lydia, the seller of purple silk, in whose house Paul found comfort in the Spirit of the Lord, had come into the Kingdom through the South Gate, and had opened her heart to God as a bud opens into flower before the summer sunshine.

Not long ago I was talking to a young boy who was contemplating becoming a minister, and I asked him to tell me of his Christian experience. He told me that his parents had prayed for him even before he was born, that he had been dedicated to God when he was only a child, and had grown up in a Christian atmosphere *charged* with prayer, so that as he grew older there was no life apart from Christ which had any appeal for him. Blessed are they who have been so trained in the home that their Christian experience has become to them something of grace and beauty. Of course, they still must accept Christ as their Saviour, but it is so much easier to accept Him if they have always been taught to love and respect Him.

IV. THE EAST GATE

Still others enter the Kingdom through the gate that faces the east. In the language of the Bible the east is the place of the desert, where the sands drift and the treeless wastes speak of the sorrow and disappointment and the loneliness of life. So it is that some come to Christ through the East Gate, led to Him by the experience of emptiness lying like a great burden on their hearts.

It was through the East Gate that the Wise Men came, when they saw the star of Jesus in the East, bringing Him gifts of gold, frankincense, and myrrh.

Today there are multitudes of people to whom life spells failure, whose hearts are empty, who face disappointed hopes and broken purposes. Suddenly they find in Christ full and complete satisfaction. He becomes to them the Bread which satisfies spiritual hunger and the Water of Life which quenches spiritual thirst.

There are many in the East who are now living in desert and sand drifts. It was out of the East that the Rich Young Ruler came to Jesus, saying, "What lack I yet? He had everything that the world could give him, yet he did not have peace. Every word that describes him is freighted with richness. He had youth, he had power and influence, he had great wealth at his disposal. He is called the Rich Young Ruler, and yet his life lacked something which neither youth nor wealth nor worldly powers could ever give to him. His cry to Jesus was, "What is lacking in my soul?"

There is no burden comparable to an empty life, and Christ comes to supply and to satisfy the deepest hunger of the heart.

If you are out there in some lonely desert and your

heart is yearning for peace and comfort and satisfaction, then I urge you to come through the East Gate to the feet of Jesus.

There is a bridge in Europe on each pier of which stands a statue of Christ. He is represented as a Shepherd, as a Sower, as a Physician, as a Pilot, and as a Carpenter. People passing and repassing pause in adoration before the Christ who holds their hearts. The sheperd waits in silence before the Christ who speaks to him as a Shepherd, the farmer before Him who is the great Sower of the Gospel seed, the sailor before the Pilot, the laborer before the Carpenter, and the sick and the sorrowful before Him who called for man's soul. The statues represent the various ways by which we are attracted to Him who is our Lord and Saviour.

Now, the one simple truth that I would leave with every one of you is this: there is a path that leads from where you are today up to the feet of Jesus. You may go through the West Gate with Paul and St. Augustine, or through the North Gate with Nicodemus and Thomas, or through the South Gate with Lydia and Timothy, or through the East Gate with Peter and Zaccheus. But no matter which way your path leads, or which gate you enter, you must go by the Way of the Cross and confess your sins at the feet of Jesus, who is still saying to every one of us, "Come unto me, all ye that labour and are heavy laden, and I will give you rest."

38. A FINE COLLECTION I

TEXT: *Add to your faith virtue; and to virtue knowledge; and to knowledge temperance.* II PETER 1:5, 6.

OBJECTS: Three small cardboard boxes, with the word "faith" printed on No. 1, "virtue" on No. 2, and "knowledge" on No. 3.

THE LESSON: Sooner or later, most boys and girls develop a hobby of collecting things which are of interest to them. It may be Indian arrowheads, butterflies, stamps, minerals, etc. Every boy and girl ought to have such a hobby; it is great fun. I have in my possession several hundred Indian arrowheads and many other Indian relics that I collected when I was much younger than I am now. Occasionally I pour these relics on a table and look at them. They remind me of the glorious days of my youth.

In the first chapter of Second Peter we find a new kind of collection suggested by the apostle. As we consider them we will find a collection of virtues, or elements of character, which will help us as we grow older:

> Add to your faith virtue; and to virtue knowl-
> edge; and to knowledge temperance; and to
> temperance patience; and to patience godli-
> ness; and to godliness brotherly kindness; and
> to brotherly kindness charity.

As we look at the virtues or elements of character represented by these boxes we will notice that one virtue grows directly out of the other.

I. FAITH. Faith in God is the foundation of all other worth-while virtues. That is true because, in the Apostle Paul's words (Hebrews 11:1), faith is the substance of things hoped for, the evidence of things not seen. When he wrote of faith, Paul evidently did not have in mind the endorsement of an inherited system of beliefs and practices or the mere approval of some Christian doctrine. The faith of which he spoke has reference to a way of life—action based on the assurance of things hoped for, the evidence of things not seen. When faith is so understood, we find ourselves faced, not so much with theological problems, as with the commonplace problems of life.

There are two popular assumptions about faith which are widely used but which, nevertheless, are false. For one thing, many people believe that faith is just blind belief that we can accomplish the impossible simply by believing what we want to believe, but Paul plainly says that faith is the assurance of things hoped for, the evidence of things not seen. There must be some basis for our hoping and some assurance that our hopes may be realized.

The second false assumption about faith holds that in matters of religion we must experience our faith in God, but in other matters make our own decisions and direct our action on the basis of knowledge. That is not true. We must live by faith every day and every hour. When we flip the light switch or take a drink of water or eat breakfast or get in our car to go somewhere, we are exercising faith in both things and people. The reason we can have faith in both things and people is simple. We have evidence to support our faith. When I flip the light switch the light comes on if there is not a loose connection or a burned-out bulb. When I sit down to eat breakfast I do not worry for fear my wife has put poison in my coffee—I have faith in her. So, by the same token, I have faith in the spoken Word of God. He promised to save me if I would accept Him as my Saviour. I took Him at His word and I believe that He will keep His promise.

(Place the second box on top of the first one.)

II. VIRTUE. Virtue is the fruit of faith. When faith becomes the foundation of our life, goodness is bound to follow. When we begin to live by doing what Jesus teaches us to do, then we are certain to become Christlike in our behavior. We tend to become like that which we love, "for as he thinketh in his heart, so is he." Goodness comes as a natural result of our faith in God. All goodness must begin in the heart where Jesus dwells, but it cannot stop there. It must move out of the heart until it becomes universal in scope.

III. KNOWLEDGE. (Place the third box on top of

the second one.) Now we have faith, virtue, and knowledge, stacked on top of each other in logical order. Knowledge is a wonderful thing. In lands where Christ is not known the people live in ignorance and superstition. Since they do not know anything about the laws of sanitation or about medicine, they die by thousands from disease and pestilence. Since they do not know how to improve their land, they are constantly faced with malnutrition and starvation. Since they do not know about the love of Jesus Christ, they do not have love and kindness in their hearts.

In *Henry VI*, Shakespeare says that ". . . ignorance is the curse of God, Knowledge the wing wherewith we fly to heaven." The Apostle Paul said, "I would not have you to be ignorant, brethren." You boys and girls are going to school to increase your knowledge about a good many things, which is fine. But as you add to your store of knowledge concerning the things that are about you, you must not forget to learn more about the nature of God.

The more we read God's Word and seek to do His will, the better we shall be able to apply any other virtue we may have gained. He who has no faith in God will have but little goodness or worth-while purpose in life. He who has no basic knowledge of love and nature of God is like a man who owns a big new automobile which has everything it needs but a motor. Faith produces virtue, and virtue becomes a cradle in which knowledge grows from infancy to maturity. "Know the truth, and the truth shall make you free."

39. A FINE COLLECTION (Continued) II

TEXT: *But let patience have her perfect work, that ye may be perfect and entire, wanting nothing.* JAMES 1:4.

OBJECTS: Three more identical cardboard boxes, with "temperance" printed on No. 4, "patience" on No. 5, and "godliness" on No. 6.

THE LESSON: Today we shall continue collecting virtues or elements of character to help us as we grow older. Last Sunday we saw how these boxes representing faith, virtue, and knowledge might help us build a foundation for the future. Today we shall add three more elements of character to our collection.

IV. TEMPERANCE. Here is another box which represents temperance. We shall place it on top of the box marked knowledge. Temperance is what we often call self-control. In order to become a fine personality you will have to learn to control your desires and impulses. There may be times when some of you may feel like saying ugly things to your parents or teacher or to someone who has irritated you, but if you are wise you will resist the temptation.

Rules, regulations, and laws are made for those who are unable to control themselves. If we do not have the ability to control ourselves from the inside, then we simply must be controlled from the outside. Temperance is the ability to control ourselves from within.

We must add self-control to knowledge, because knowledge without self-control can become very dangerous. I know a young man who wanted to be a great opera singer. He worked hard and gained much knowledge concerning great music, but he never learned to control his temper. When an audience failed to respond to his singing as he thought it should, he would lose his temper and scold the people severely. His lack of self-control completely barred him from what might have been a great career in opera.

The presence of Jesus Christ in the human heart will do more than anything else to add temperance or self-control to knowledge. After we have learned to control our tempers, passions, desires, and impulses, we are then ready to add patience to temperance.

V. PATIENCE. This fifth box represents patience. We shall place it on the top of the box marked temperance, because that is where it logically belongs. After we have learned to master ourselves, we then learn to be patient with other people. The Bible has much to say about patience.

In the eighteenth chapter of Matthew, Jesus tells the story of a servant who owed a debt he could not pay, and, falling on his knees before his master, said, "Have patience with me, and I will pay thee all."

In the twenty-first chapter of Luke Jesus says, "In your patience possess ye your souls." Again, in Romans 5, Paul says, ". . . that we through patience and comfort of the scriptures might have hope. Now the God of patience and consolation grant you to be like-minded one toward another according to Christ Jesus.

In a day when all life is geared to high speed patience seems to have the irritating gait of the horse and buggy days. But let us remember that God cannot be hurried. It took Moses forty years to lead the children of Israel to the Promised Land, and the years were not wasted. God did not let the Israelites enter the Promised Land until they were ready for the new responsibility. If they had gone straight from Egypt to the Promised Land it certainly would not have taken many months to make the journey. But they were not ready for the new experience. It took forty years of ups and downs and hardships and heartaches before they were actually ready to assume their new responsibilities.

If you have not received the things for which you have been praying, be patient. Put your trust in God and wait on Him. "Let patience have her perfect work, that ye may be perfect and entire, wanting nothing" (James 1:4).

VI. GODLINESS. When we have added patience to temperance we are ready to add the sixth virtue, which is godliness. A godlike person is one whose knowledge of God, of self-control and patience have developed in him a character which is more like the character of Jesus Christ. Of course, no one can ever become as perfect or as sinless as was Jesus, but there are many ways in which we can become more like Him.

We can become more like Christ in our attitude toward forgiveness. His enemies crucified Him, but He forgave them and prayed for them even while He hung on the cross. We can at least forgive those who have only wounded us. We can also be more like Jesus in our faith in God and in the future. We have a tendency to become discouraged about human nature, but, somehow, Jesus never lost faith in human nature. The people with whom He came in contact hurt Him, they disappointed Him, they did all manner of evil things to Him, and, finally, they nailed Him to a cross, but, somehow, Jesus never did lose confidence in humanity. He believed to the end that there was always something deep and abiding in the human heart—something which would respond to love and kindness.

Next Sunday, when we complete this series of object sermons on collecting things, we shall see how important it is to include the whole collection that Peter recommended.

40. A FINE COLLECTION (Continued) III

TEXT: *Love never faileth.* I CORINTHIANS 13:8.

OBJECTS: Two more identical cardboard boxes with "brotherly kindness" printed on No. 7 and "love" on No. 8.

THE LESSON: This morning we complete our collection of virtues or elements of character as suggested by the Apostle Peter, and see what an important collection it is. Not one of the qualities represented by these seven boxes can be eliminated from our character without serious damage to the soul. (Briefly go over them all and show how essential each one is.)

VII. BROTHERLY KINDNESS. (Place box No. 7 on top of the other boxes.) Now let us place brotherly kindness on top of godliness and see how essential it is to the collection. If we have godliness or Christlikeness in our nature, we simply cannot eliminate brotherly kindness without destroying the very thing which has made us more like Christ. Sometimes brothers and sisters quarrel and find fault with one another, but in spite of these outbreaks the family tie holds them together. They have the same parents, the same love and care, and are bound together by common interests. There were ten children in my family and there were times when we had our family quarrels and would call each other ugly names; but if somebody outside the family called one of us an ugly name we would quickly unite to defend the family honor. If anything from outside the family circle hurt one member of the family, it hurt us all. In spite of the frequent family quarrels, the spirit of brotherly kindness existed in the circle.

There is a form of kindness which is not brotherly. My twelve-year-old daughter has a little Boston bull named Tag. Tag and I are great friends. I have taught him lots of tricks. When I ask him whether he had rather be married or dead, he falls over and plays dead until I gently explain to him that he does not have to get married. Then he appears to be very happy as he waits for his reward.

While I am as kind to Tag as he is to me, I do not think of him as a brother. He cannot share with me any of my dreams or heartaches or aspirations. I expect to meet my parents in heaven some day. Tag has not the least interest concerning his parents. If we were to meet his mother on the street, he would probably growl at her and then move on. I dream of great things for my daughter, but Tag cannot dream of anything more important than a bone. While we can be kind to each other, we cannot be brotherly.

Since God is our Father and we are His children, we should exercise brotherly kindness to one another. We are made in the image of God and can share with each other our dreams and our hopes and our aspirations. We cannot recognize God as our Father without also recognizing that all His children are our brothers and sisters. Brotherly kindness is the natural result of such recognition.

VIII. LOVE. As we complete this list of virtues we will notice that love is the essence of the whole collection. Love is the greatest power in all the world. Hate can cause wars and destruction, but only love can bring peace and happiness.

In John Mansfield's book, *The Trial of Jesus*, the wife of Pontius Pilate asked the centurion in charge of the crucifixion, "What do you think of His claim?" The centurion replied, "If a man believes anything up to the point of dying on a cross for it, he will find others who will believe it." Still curious, she asked, "Do you believe that He is dead?" To this the captain of the guard replied, "No, lady, I don't."

"Where is He then?" she cries, and the guard answers, "Let loose in the world, lady, where neither Roman nor Jew can stop His truths."

A story is told of a little boy named John who had lived in an orphan home as long as he could remember. Repeatedly John had seen people come to the home and adopt other children and take them away, and he always wished that somebody would come and adopt him. But always it seemed that nobody wanted him.

One day a big car with liveried chauffeur stopped at the curb. The man and woman in the big car asked John if he would like to be their little boy. They told of the many fine things they could give him, while he stood and listened in silence. Then looking up into the face of the woman who had proposed to adopt him, he said, "If you have nothing more to offer than fine clothing, a fine home, fine toys, and such things as that, I think I would prefer to remain here."

The woman, quite visibly startled, gasped, "Well, what on earth do you want?"

"You see, lady," the boy replied, "I want someone to love me."

The woman took him in her arms and said, "If that is what you want, I will love you now and forever."

I think Jesus would rather have us love Him than have anything else that we can possibly offer Him. I believe that if He were to speak to you right now He would say, "I want you to love me." If you love Jesus, you will strive to do His will, and then He will love you both now and forever.

This is a fine collection of virtues and I hope you will begin with faith and add to your collection until you have them all stored up in your heart.